The

Reboot
with Joe

JUICE DIET
COOKBOOK

**JUICE, SMOOTHIE AND PLANT-BASED RECIPES
INSPIRED BY THE HIT DOCUMENTARY
*FAT, SICK & NEARLY DEAD***

JOE CROSS

GREENLEAF
BOOK GROUP PRESS

Published by Greenleaf Book Group Press
Austin, Texas
www.gbgpress.com

Distributed by Greenleaf Book Group

For ordering information or special discounts for bulk purchases, please contact Greenleaf Book Group at PO Box 91869, Austin, TX 78709, 512.891.6100.

Design and composition by Greenleaf Book Group
Cover design by Greenleaf Book Group
Cover Photograph by Richard Lohr Studios
Interior Photographs by Daniel Krieger

Cataloging-in-Publication data

Cross, Joe.
The Reboot with Joe Juice Diet Cookbook: Juices, Smoothies and Plant-based Recipes Inspired by the Hit Documentary Fat, Sick, and Nearly Dead/ Joe Cross.—1st ed.
p. ; cm.
Companion to book titled The Reboot with Joe juice diet.
Includes bibliographical references and index.
ISBN: 978-1-62634-137-1
1. Vegetable juices. 2. Fruit juices 3. Smoothies (Beverages) 4. Reducing diets--Recipes.
5. Cookbooks. I. Companion to (work) Cross, Joe. Reboot with Joe juice diet. II. Title.
III. Title: Inspired by (work) Fat, sick, and nearly dead.
TX840.J84 C76 2014
641.875   2014939965

Part of the Tree Neutral® program, which offsets the number of trees consumed in the production and printing of this book by taking proactive steps, such as planting trees in direct proportion to the number of trees used: www.treeneutral.com

TreeNeutral

Printed in Canada on acid-free paper

18 19 20 21 22 23   11 10 9 8 7 6 5 4

First Edition

ACKNOWLEDGMENTS

Thank you to the Reboot Team—Kari Thorstensen, Amie Hannon, Brenna Ryan, Jamie Schneider, Sophie Carrel, Chris Zilo, Ameet Matura, Alex Tibbetts, Erin Flowers, Sarah Mawson, Sean Frechette, Vernon Caldwell, Jamin Mendelsohn, Kurt Engfehr, Shane Hodson, Stacy Kennedy, and Claire Georgiou—who, regardless of their jobs, all take delight in creating and taste testing new and delicious Reboot-friendly recipes. Their work is in these pages.

Thank you to the Reboot with Joe Medical Advisory Board (in addition to Stacy Kennedy)—Ronald Penny MD, DSc, Carrie Diulus MD, and Adrian Rawlinson MD—who continue to endorse and advocate for Rebooting as an effective means to achieve weight loss and health and always endeavor to keep me straight on my facts.

Thank you to Sarah Hammond and the team at Hodder & Stoughton for their suggestion to do this book and their guidance and enthusiasm in bringing it to market along with the team at Greenleaf Book Group.

CONTENTS

INTRODUCTION

Seventy percent of all disease is caused by lifestyle choices.[1]

Let me say that again.

Seventy percent of all disease is caused by lifestyle choices.

What are those "choices," you ask? Well, the big three are whether you smoke, how much you exercise, and what you eat and drink. It's pretty clear that if you make good choices (don't smoke, exercise consistently, and eat healthy foods), you'll be on the right side of the fight against disease. But sometimes making those good choices is harder than you think. It's become normal—average, even—to be overweight in our society. And pretty average to be managing a chronic illness by taking medication. In that case, I was just an average bloke.

A few years ago, on the cusp of forty, I took a long, hard look in the mirror and wasn't pleased with what was looking back at me—a lifetime of not-good choices (OK, fine—pretty terrible choices) had taken their predictable toll. I was chronically ill and almost 100 pounds overweight. But instead of registering nothing but shock and horror, I saw a silver lining—it was 70 percent likely that I had caused this myself. And if that were the case, I had a pretty good chance of fixing it myself, too. In order to do that, I needed to enlist the help of Mother Nature, so I decided to consume nothing but the juice of fresh fruits and vegetables for 60 days. I chronicled this in the documentary *Fat, Sick & Nearly Dead*.

I had created a vicious cycle for myself, and as I stood there looking in the mirror on the eve of my milestone birthday, I realized that if I didn't make a radical change, I would squander the incredible gifts I had been given and wind up

---

1   "Preventable illness makes up approximately 70 percent of the burden of illness and the associated costs. Well-developed national statistics such as those outlined in *Healthy People 2000, Health U.S. 1991*, and elsewhere document this central fact clearly." James F. Fries, C. Everett Koop, Carson E. Beadle, Paul P. Cooper, Mary Jane England, Roger F. Greaves, Jacque J. Sokolov, Daniel Wright, and the Health Project Consortium, "Reducing Health Care Costs by Reducing the Need and Demand for Medical Services." *New England Journal of Medicine* 329 (July 29, 1993): 321–325. doi:/full/10.1056/NEJM199307293290506

in an early grave. When it finally dawned on me that perhaps I was the problem, let me tell you, that was a pretty sobering moment—it's hard to acknowledge that you are the agent of your own destruction, and it's pretty embarrassing too.

I had turned my back on Mother Nature and ignored the simple but powerful lesson that we are taught as young children. Eat your vegetables and fruits. This may sound simplistic, but at the time I had only the most glancing relationship with green vegetables—they were the things I moved to the side to get to the things I actually wanted—and "fruit" was most often the maraschino cherry atop a sundae or a handful of berries that were decorating a plate of *real* dessert. What if I took my consumption of fruits and vegetables from almost zero to 100 percent? That would be a pretty straightforward experiment and would yield a definitive conclusion, right? But how to do it? The thought of eating pounds and pounds of plant-based foods every day was daunting, and as anyone who has known me for 10 minutes will attest, I'm a guy in a hurry. It occurred to me that the most speedy and efficient method of flooding my system with nutrients would be to juice vegetables and fruits and consume nothing but that juice for a period of time. My hope was that it would reboot my system and return me to the state of good health I had known as a boy.

By the end of my journey, I was medication free, had lost the 100 pounds, and felt absolutely like new. I'd been given a fresh lease on life. I decided to use the extra time and energy I had to try to help people just like me see that there was an effective, simple way to reclaim their well-being and vitality. The intervening few years have so far surpassed my expectations that it's almost comical. *Fat, Sick & Nearly Dead* has, at the time of this writing, been seen by more than 11 million people around the world. My efforts to spread information and encouragement coalesced into a business and an online community, Reboot with Joe (www.rebootwithjoe.com), where millions of people have received the tools, recipes, and community they needed to Reboot their lives. I've lectured all over the world and have been moved, inspired, and humbled by the stories of personal transformation that people from Auckland to Oakland have shared with me.

My last book, *The Reboot with Joe Juice Diet*, became a great success very quickly, in part because people who had been inspired by the film wanted to know how they could adapt the plan I followed to fit their own lives. We put together a group of plans that offered different ways to Reboot, allowing people to choose the Reboot plan that best suited their lifestyle. Now, one of the advantages of having an online community is that you get customer feedback immediately and without a filter. What I started to hear from Rebooters (I reckon you may be one of them!) who had followed the plans in my how-to book was twofold.

The first? "More, please."

So I've written this book for those of you who want MORE—more recipes, more support, more information, and more variety. Whether it's your first Reboot, or your fourteenth, what you're about to read will help you reset your palate, clear away the cobwebs, and take responsibility for your health and well-being. And you'll find that this information has value beyond the period of your Reboot—I think it will help you incorporate the behaviors, recipes, and choices that make this lifestyle permanent. This book is a companion to your Reboot plan (if you don't have one, pick up a copy of the *Reboot with Joe Juice Diet* book or visit www.rebootwithjoe.com). You can use all the recipes in this book as a substitute for the recipes on the Reboot plans—so you can customize your period of entirely plant-based eating and juicing to your taste! We've even color-coded the recipes to ensure that with any substitutions you are still getting a variety of vitamins and minerals. You can also take into account any health conditions, since we've listed those that are improved by a particular juice next to the relevant recipe. And if you're post-Reboot, well, I reckon these are just great recipes to have on hand to combine with your favorite healthy grains or meat, or to enjoy on their own!

And the next is, "What now?"

Well, my answer to "What now?" is *Fat, Sick & Nearly Dead 2*, which is being released in the fall of 2014. It addresses the next stage of the lifelong journey that follows a decision to change—one that I'm excited to share with you. If you want to find out how to see the film when it debuts, be sure to visit us at RebootwithJoe.com and sign up for our newsletter.

You see, I got lucky. I stumbled onto a simple solution that had profound results. As far as I'm concerned, Rebooting saved my life—not just by adding years to my life but also by returning me to a state of being that is characterized by joy more than by despair and by a sense of possibility that is far more potent than the threat of a doomed ending. And it can do the same for you, if you're lucky. I have a saying: "Lady Luck follows a person of action." I hope this book helps you take action.

Juice on!

Joe Cross
August 2014

HOW TO USE THIS BOOK

This book is meant to accompany a Reboot—a period of time in which you consume only fresh fruits and vegetables. I am assuming that you have already decided on a Reboot plan and are already Rebooting or ready to go. If you don't have a plan, you can find some, for free, on my website RebootwithJoe.com. These same plans, along with tons of information about how Rebooting works and how to successfully Reboot, are also available in my book *The Reboot with Joe Juice Diet*.

I hope this new recipe book will provide inspiration to you help keep your Reboot fresh and interesting. You may be tired of drinking my Mean Green juice, or maybe you are not really a fan of the Roasted Acorn Squash Stuffed with Mushroom and Sage. That's OK. This recipe book will provide you with additional recipes that you can substitute for any of those on the Reboot plans, enabling you to customize your Reboot to your liking or to include what is seasonally fresh and available.

You can substitute any smoothie for one listed in the book, any salad for another salad recipe here, and so on. We've color-coded the juices—red, orange, green, purple, and yellow. Try substituting with a like color to make sure you are getting a variety of vitamins and minerals. If you have a health condition, pay attention to those listed by the recipe—this tells you which juices are particularly helpful for each condition. If you have diabetes or a thyroid condition, extra care should be paid when consuming raw juice and foods; please check out the sections on Rebooting for Diabetes and Rebooting for Thyroid Conditions for more information.

And if you're not Rebooting? The recipes in this book are an excellent way to keep your diet full of fruits and veggies. So feel free to combine these with your favorite grains and meat, or enjoy the mains for a meatless feast.

The recipes here are a collection of old favorites as well as some new ones that we created just for this book. For more recipe inspiration, community, and tools to help you with your Reboot, check out RebootwithJoe.com.

KEY

Season: The ideal season in the Northern Hemisphere for one or more key items in the recipe, to help you get produce at its best.

Color: Try to drink a variety of colors. If substituting on a Reboot plan, substitute color for like color.

🕐 This is a quick and easy item to make, using few ingredients or elaborate preparation.

🏃 Great for post-workout—or if it's a juice, even during your workout.

➕ Especially helpful if you have one or more of the listed health conditions.

R Appropriate for a Reboot (which all the recipes in this book are, except for some of the pulp recipes).

REBOOT DAILY GUIDE

On juicing-only days your fluid intake should look like this. Substitute other juices based on the color indicated next to the recipe.

- Wake up: 9 fl oz/250 ml hot water with lemon and/or ginger
- Breakfast: Go Orange or Red
- Mid-morning: Drink 16 fl oz/500 ml coconut water
- Lunch: Go Green
- Afternoon snack: Go Yellow or Red
- Dinner: Go Green
- Dessert: Go Purple or Orange
- Bedtime: Drink herbal tea
- Throughout the day: Drink lots of water (48 fl oz/1.5 liters)

JUICING

How to make a juice

Wash produce thoroughly. Unwashed fruit and vegetables can be contaminated with bacteria, so washing is an important step in the juicing process.

Line your juicer's pulp basket. If your juicer has a pulp basket, line it with a plastic bag so that cleaning it is easy. Look for biodegradable bags that you can throw straight into the compost along with your pulp. Remember that pulp can also be used to boost the nutritional and fiber content of certain recipes. Visit page 203 and www.rebootwithjoe.com for more tips on what to do with your pulp, from composting to making broth and baking muffins.

Cut or tear produce to size. It must be able to fit through the juicer's feeder tube, so cut any produce that might be too large to fit. Remember, this is best done just before juicing.

Feed produce through the juicer's feeder tube. If your machine has more than one speed, don't forget to downshift from high to low for soft fruits (the instruction manual should be able to guide you about speeds). Usually, hard types of produce, such as apples and beets (beetroot), are juiced on high, while soft ones, such as spinach and cabbage, are set to low.

Re-juice your pulp. Once produce has been passed through the juicer, check to see if the pulp is still damp. If it is, pass it back through the juicer, and you'll be able to get more juice from it.

Drink up. At this point, you should have a fresh juice ready to drink. If you prefer it cold, pour over ice, but whatever the case, drink it as soon as possible because once it's juiced, it starts to lose its nutritional value. If stored properly (see page 12), it can last 2–3 days, but remember that there are no preservatives in fresh juice (which is why we love it), so it can quickly go bad.

Now it's time to clean your juicer. Carefully scrub the machine with warm water and soap and place on a drying mat. If it's dishwasher friendly (check the manual), you'll have an even easier clean.

EAT THE RAINBOW

Eat the rainbow sounds like a fun way to eat, but what does it mean? It means over the course of a day, mix it up, eat a variety of colors, and over a week eat a variety of different whites, yellows, oranges, reds, greens, and purples (the juicing rainbow).

Orange fruits and vegetables, such as carrots and oranges, get their vibrant hue from beta-carotene and an abundance of antioxidants, vitamins, fiber, and phytonutrients that are good for your skin, eyes, and heart. They also contain high amounts of vitamin A that helps protect your body against free radicals and vitamin C that helps boost the immune system.

Red fruits and vegetables like beets (beetroots) and cherries are high in anthocyanins (antioxidants) and offer a host of vitamins, minerals, and other antioxidants that can help your body fight off disease and stay healthy. Beets in particular contain a nutrient called betalain, which has been shown to provide antioxidants, and help promote anti-inflammation, and they are excellent for pre-workouts because they help bring more oxygen to the blood.

Leafy greens, my favorites, are super high in chlorophyll and give me the energy to keep going forever! Not to mention the extreme concentration of phytonutrients, vitamins, and minerals needed to function properly. Now think about it, if you combine all these colors, you'll help your body stay strong and healthy.

Tips for storing juice

Place in an airtight container. Glass is ideal, but BPA-free plastic works, too. Some authorities, such as the US Food and Drug Administration, advise against Bisphenol-A (BPA), an industrial chemical often used in the manufacturing of plastic. Some research studies have linked BPA to breast cancer and diabetes, as well as to hyperactivity, aggression, and depression in children.[2]

Fill the container to the top. This will prevent oxygen from getting in, which can deplete the nutrients.

Keep for 2 to 3 days in the fridge (72 hours is the maximum time suggested). If you are traveling, take your juice in a cooler. Do not use an aluminum Thermos or vacuum flask because metal can react with the juice.

Freeze it for up to 10 days. If you will not be drinking the juice within 48 hours, it is best to freeze it immediately. Thaw in the refrigerator when needed. Make sure you drink the whole amount within 10 days of freezing.

To peel or not to peel?

I love lemon peel in my juice but have to admit that I seem to be a bit unusual. If I am making my Mean Green for a first-time juicer, I leave out the peel because I don't want to scare anyone away from juicing. But in a citrus fruit, there are over sixty flavonoids, with the highest concentration being in the peel. (Flavonoids are

---

2 Frederick S. vom Saal and John Peterson Myers, "Bisphenol A and Risk of Metabolic Disorders," *The Journal of the American Medical Association*, 2008; 300(11): 1353–1355.

Iain A. Lang, Tamara S. Galloway, Alan Scarlett, et al., "Association of Urinary Bisphenol A Concentration with Medical Disorders and Laboratory Abnormalities in Adults," *The Journal of the American Medical Association*, 2008; 300(11): 1303–1310.

"Our conclusions are consistent with the large number of hazards and adverse effects identified in laboratory animals exposed to low doses of BPA." L.N. Vandenberg, P. A. Hunt, J. P. Myers, F. S. Vom Saal, "Human Exposures to Bisphenol A: Mismatches between Data and Assumptions." *Reviews on Environmental Health*, 2013; 28(1): 37–58.

substances found in plants, many of which are responsible for the yellow, orange, and red pigmentation. And they're really good for you.) The pith—the white part right under the peel on a citrus fruit—also contains lots of nutrients. So if you really can't handle the peel in your juice, try to leave on the pith. In this case, I recommend cutting off the peel so you can leave on more of the pith.

In general, the outer layers of fruits and vegetables often provide more nutrition than the food they protect. Gram for gram, citrus peels also contain higher levels of many minerals and vitamins, such as vitamin C, and dietary fiber than the fruit's flesh. For example, one tablespoon of lemon peel contains double the amount of vitamin C and triple the amount of fiber of one wedge of lemon without the peel, according to the United States Department of Agriculture (USDA) database. So for most fruits and vegetables, leave the peels on. Here are a few other peels and skins you might not think you could juice—but you can.

WATERMELON

Watermelon rind is excellent for juicing—it is lower in sugar content than the flesh and higher in potassium and dietary fiber. If you are throwing away the rind, you are discarding not only about 40 percent of the fresh weight of the watermelon but also a potent source of citrulline. Citrulline is an amino acid that is converted to arginine in the body. Arginine increases blood flow, which decreases blood pressure and improves overall cardiovascular health.

As with citrus fruits, the white part of the rind is full of nutrients. If the whole rind is too much flavor for your juice, try leaving some of the white rind on the watermelon flesh when you cut it up.

MANGOES

Don't skin mangoes before you juice them. This part of the fruit contains a significant number of antioxidants and healthful compounds that are found only in small amounts in the mango pulp. Mangiferin, a phytonutrient found in large amounts in the skin, is a powerful antioxidant. Mangiferin may be helpful in protecting against skin cancer, and its UV-protectant ability is valued in the cosmetics industry. Of course, don't skip the SPF!

Beware of mango itch! While mango skin is edible, be careful because it can cause an allergic reaction in some people. Known as "mango itch" in Hawaii, the sap of the mango tree and mango skin contains urushiol, the same compound responsible for the itchy skin rash seen in poison ivy and poison oak. People who are sensitive to poison ivy and poison oak may also be sensitive to the urushiol in mangoes and should avoid eating or juicing the skin.

APPLES

Apples might be a little more obvious to you since it's common to eat them with the skins on, but you'd be surprised to know that many people prefer to eat apples after peeling off the skin. If you're one of them, you might want to reconsider because the majority of the apple's nutrients are found in the peel. The peel is loaded with vitamins A and C, and heaps of minerals like calcium, potassium, and iron. Let's not forget about the fiber! About two-thirds of an apple's fiber, both soluble and insoluble, exists in its peel.

With any peels, if you do juice or eat them, it is best to use organic products because the peel is where pesticide residue can be concentrated. Whether you purchase organic or not, be sure to wash your fruits well before juicing, blending, or eating them. Try a homemade wash with vinegar, lemon, bicarbonate of soda (baking soda), and water to help remove pesticide residue.

- Citrus peels—Zest or grate citrus peels to infuse their essence into smoothies and baked goods. Grated or fine chopped peels also add a bright flavoring to savory dishes and sauces.

- Mango peels—Mangoes can be eaten raw with their skin on, though some people may not like the texture or think the taste is bitter. If you find that to be the case, cut up the mango with its skin and blend in a high-powered blender, mixing with other fruits and vegetables. Choose some of the thinner-skinned varieties and make sure the fruit is ripe, as that is when the skin is at its thinnest. Mango skin can be pickled, or it can be sun- or oven-dried to make a crunchy chip.

- Watermelon rind—Instead of throwing the white rind away, leave some of it attached when you cut up the watermelon flesh. You can juice the watermelon this way or add it to smoothies. If you find the result a little bitter, the addition of sweet fruits and/or spices such as fresh ginger will offset this. Pickled watermelon rind is also a classic southern alternative to pickles in the US.

- Apples—Rinse well before eating and then bite right into it, or slice it up in smaller pieces and top with your favorite nut butter for a heartier snack.

- Leek leaves—Did you know that leeks are one of the most iron-rich plant foods—they contain more iron than spinach! I've always thrown away the leaf—the dark green part of the leek at the top—in favor of the white and light green parts. (No, it's not a peel; it's something we typically throw away and shouldn't!) I was always told that the dark green parts weren't edible. Boy, was I told wrong. While the green leaves are thicker than the shaft of the leek, they need only a little time to cook. The secret is to slice them fairly thin, in rounds or strips. Slicing diagonally is another helpful trick. Braise them in a little stock, or sauté them in a little oil over medium heat until lightly browned and use as a garnish. Chop them up and add them to your vegetables when making stocks. If you blanch them first (to make them malleable), you can also use the leaves as the outer layer in rolls with tofu, fish, or other protein, infusing them with a mild oniony flavor.

Juicing produce preparation guide

Not sure what to do with those fruits, veggies, and spices before you put them in your juicer? Here's a list of how to prepare the most commonly used ingredients. Once you've gained confidence by making the juices in this book, get creative and start experimenting with your own combinations. You can also find more juice recipes at www.rebootwithjoe.com/recipes.

VEGETABLES	HOW TO PREPARE
Asparagus	Rinse the spears (stalks) carefully and push through the juicer, bottom first.
Aubergine	see Eggplant
Beets	Peel if you wish to avoid the earthy taste that many people dislike, and cut to fit your juicer. Juice the beet greens too.
Beetroot	see Beets
Bell peppers	see Sweet (bell) peppers
Broccoli	After rinsing, juice all parts.
Butterhead lettuce	Rinse leaves individually, checking for dirt and sand. No need to remove the stems. Roll the leaves up and feed into the juicer, following each batch with a harder fruit or vegetable, such as apple, celery, or cucumber, to help them pass through.
Cabbage, green and red	The cabbage head should be firm with crisp leaves. Cut into quarters, or smaller if necessary to fit into the juicer's feeder tube.

VEGETABLES	HOW TO PREPARE
Capsicum	*see* Sweet (bell) peppers
Carrots	Rinse thoroughly before passing through the juicer. No need to peel them or to discard the greens.
Celeriac	*see* Celery root
Celery	Rinse thoroughly and pass the entire celery stalk, including leaves, through the juicer.
Celery root	Wash carefully, as grit can get stuck in the nooks and crannies. As with beets, if you don't like an earthy taste, peel the celery root first. Cut to fit your juicer.
Chard	Rinse leaves individually, checking for dirt and sand. No need to remove the stems. Roll up and feed into the juicer, following each batch with a harder fruit or vegetable, such as apple, celery, or cucumber, to help them pass through.
Collard greens	Wash the leaves. No need to remove the stems. Roll up and feed into the juicer, following each batch with a harder fruit or vegetable, such as apple, celery, or cucumber, to help them pass through.
Cos lettuce	*see* Romaine lettuce
Courgettes	*see* Zucchini
Cucumbers	Cut in half. No need to peel.
Dandelion greens	Wash the leaves. No need to remove the stems. Roll up and feed into the juicer, following each batch with a harder fruit or vegetable, such as apple, celery, or cucumber, to help them pass through. Dandelion greens have some bite to them, so use sparingly, or soften the flavor with a sweet and juicy fruit such as pineapple.
Eggplant	I've never juiced an eggplant and don't think I ever will.
Fennel	Rinse and then chop the bulb to fit through the juicer. You can also juice the fronds for extra nutrients. Fennel has a light aniseed flavor, which reminds me of licorice.
Jicama	Wash and slice, but don't peel. The resulting juice will contain nutrients that were near the skin even after the skin has been pulped away.
Kai choi	*see* Mustard greens

VEGETABLES	HOW TO PREPARE
Kale	Use any kind—lacinato, red, green, purple, curly, etc. Wash the leaves, roll up 3–4 at a time, and feed into the juicer, following each batch with a harder fruit or vegetable, such as apple, celery, or cucumber, to help them pass through.
Kohlrabi	Both leaves and bulb can be juiced, but the flavor (similar to broccoli) is strong, so aim for a juice that contains no more than 25 percent kohlrabi.
Leeks	Trim off the woody base and then slice both green and white parts in half lengthways. Gently separate the layers and rinse between them.
Mexican turnip	*see Jicama*
Mustard greens	Use just a small amount, as they have a strong flavor that will literally warm your insides. Wash the leaves. No need to remove the stems. Roll up and feed into the juicer, following each batch with a harder fruit or vegetable, such as apple, celery, or cucumber, to help them pass through.
Onions	Go easy on these, as they can give your juices a super-strong flavor. Some people prefer not to juice them at all, especially if raw onion upsets their stomach. Peel off the papery skin and then chop to fit into your juicer. Add to your juice a little at a time, tasting as you go and adding more if you like it.
Parsnips	Rinse thoroughly before passing through the juicer. No need to peel them. You might need to slice large ones in half lengthways. These can be used to help push leafy greens through your juicer.
Pumpkin	*see Squashes*
Radishes	Leave the roots and stems on, but discard the leaves if they have any. Rinse and run through your juicer. Watch out! These can spice up your juice in a flash, so add small amounts at a time. If you're feeling cold, adding these to your juice will warm you right up.
Romaine lettuce	Rinse leaves individually, checking for dirt and sand. No need to remove the stems. Roll up and feed into the juicer, following each batch with a harder fruit or vegetable, such as apple, celery, or cucumber, to help them pass through.
Scallions	Just rinse and juice. No need to remove the roots or dark green parts because you can juice it all. These have a strong flavor like onions, so start small.

VEGETABLES	HOW TO PREPARE
Silver beet	*see* Chard
Spring onions	*see* Scallions
Spinach	Wash well—some bunches can have a lot of grit on them. No need to remove the stems. Roll up and feed into the juicer, following each batch with a harder fruit or vegetable, such as apple, celery, or cucumber, to help them pass through.
Squashes (including pumpkin)	Remove the stem and scrub the skin. If the skin is really tough and thick, you might want to peel it. Otherwise, slice with the seeds in (they provide extra cancer-fighting chemicals), and pass through the juicer.
Sugar snap peas	Rinse and run through the juicer. These don't have a very high water content, so they don't yield a lot of juice. Try juicing them with carrots.
Sweet (bell) peppers	Rinse and then remove the stem—it's fine to retain the seeds. Cut to size and juice.
Sweet potatoes	Scrub and cut into chunks. Combine them with peaches, pears, and/or apples, and you'll have a delicious dessert juice.
Tomatoes	Wash and then remove the stem and any leaves. Keep the seeds. If large, slice to fit your juicer. Fresh tomato juice is worlds away from the canned stuff.
Turnips	Scrub and chop into chunks to fit your juicer. A great addition to a juice for cooler weather.
Tuscan cabbage	*see* Kale
Wheatgrass	Some juicers are better at doing wheatgrass than others. If you're preparing just a small amount, any kind of juicer should be able to handle it. Rinse the wheatgrass, twist or roll it into a ball, and push it through the machine with something juicy and firm, such as apples. Adding wheatgrass will give a strong green flavor to the juice and provide lots of great chlorophyll energy.
Yam bean	*see* Jicama
Zucchini	Scrub and cut off stem, but leave the rounded end on. These are great for pushing through leafy greens.

FRUITS	HOW TO PREPARE
Apples	Core and remove the seeds before pushing through the juicer.
Apricots	Rinse and slice in half to remove the pit.
Avocados	Peel and remove the pit—easily lifted out with a spoon. The flesh is great for thickening juices in a blender, but never put an avocado in a juicer.
Bananas	Peel, but never juice bananas. Like avocados, they are great for thickening juices in a blender.
Blackberries	Rinse in a strainer. They don't keep well after being rinsed, so wash them the day you plan to juice them.
Blueberries	Rinse in a strainer.
Cactus pears	*see* Prickly pears
Chayotes	Wash and chop to size. No need to peel or to remove seed.
Cherries	Remove stems and then rinse the fruit. Use a small paring knife to remove the pits before juicing.
Chochos	*see* Chayotes
Cranberries	Rinse and pass through the juicer. Make sure you juice them with something sweet because these are really tart, not like ready-made cranberry juice.
Grapefruit	Peel thin, keeping as much of the white pith on the fruit as possible (it contains nutrients that help the body absorb the vitamin C and amazing antioxidants found in citrus fruits). Cut to fit the juicer and remove the seeds. If you have a centrifugal juicer, you can keep the seeds in: they contain excellent nutrients too.
Grapes	Wash and remove from their stems. Pass them through the juicer. Experiment with different colors because they yield different flavors.
Kiwi fruit	Peel and run through the juicer, seeds and all.
Kumquats	Juice whole.
Lemons	Peel thin, keeping as much of the white pith on the fruit as possible (it contains nutrients that help the body absorb the vitamin C and amazing antioxidants found in citrus fruits). Cut to fit the juicer and remove the seeds. If you have a centrifugal juicer, you can keep the seeds in: they contain excellent nutrients too.

FRUITS	HOW TO PREPARE
Limes	Peel thin, keeping as much of the white pith on the fruit as possible (it contains nutrients that help the body absorb the vitamin C and amazing antioxidants found in citrus fruits). Cut to fit the juicer and remove the seeds. If you have a centrifugal juicer, you can keep the seeds in: they contain excellent nutrients too.
Mangoes	Peel and cut spears of flesh by making angled incisions down to the large, flat pit in the middle. Makes a great tropical juice when mixed with pineapple. Also imparts a great creamy texture.
Melons	Cantaloupe has orange flesh, which should be cut into wedges and then peeled and deseeded before juicing. Other types of melon (e.g., Charentais, Galia, and Honeydew) can be juiced with their seeds.
Oranges	Peel thin, keeping as much of the white pith on the fruit as possible (it contains nutrients that help the body absorb the vitamin C and amazing antioxidants found in citrus fruits). Cut to fit the juicer and remove the seeds. If you have a centrifugal juicer, you can keep the seeds in: they contain excellent nutrients too.
Papayas	Cut in half and peel off the skin. The seeds can be juiced with the flesh.
Peaches	Cut in half to remove the pit. Then pass through the juicer.
Pears	Remove the stem. Then wash and juice whole. Slice to fit your juicer if necessary.
Pineapples	The heavier the pineapple, the riper it is. Grab hold of the top and twist off (you might want to wear gloves for this). Slice into quarters, cut out the woody core, peel off the skin, and juice.
Plums	Wash and slice in half to remove the pit. I love experimenting with different types of plums—there are so many. They give your juice a gorgeous color with an antioxidant punch.
Pomegranates	I have a great trick for dealing with this fruit. Fill a bowl with water and then slice the pomegranate in half, keeping the halves together. Submerge it in the water and then break it apart—this prevents the juice from squirting everywhere. Keeping it in the water, break the pomegranate into chunks and tease the seeds out. The white parts and skin will float, and the seeds will sink. Discard all the skin and white parts from the surface of the water, and use a slotted spoon to lift out the seeds. Juice them in their entirety.
Prickly pears	Wear gloves when handling these if the spines have not already been removed. Peel and cut to size if necessary.

FRUITS	HOW TO PREPARE
Raspberries	Rinse and juice. I love to add a little bit of lemon to a juice made with raspberries, or combine them with fresh peaches for a peach melba juice.
Strawberries	As these have a powerful flavor when juiced, I like to mix them with other berries, or maybe one or two other fruits. Just rinse, discard the leafy bits, and pop right into the juicer.
Tangerines	Peel thin, keeping as much of the white pith on the fruit as possible (it contains nutrients that help the body absorb the vitamin C and amazing antioxidants found in citrus fruits). Cut to fit the juicer and remove the seeds. If you have a centrifugal juicer, you can keep the seeds in: they contain excellent nutrients too.
Watermelon	Makes an amazingly refreshing juice, especially in hot weather. Simply cut into wedges and juice the rind, flesh, and seeds.

HERBS AND SPICES	HOW TO PREPARE
Basil	Wash carefully, swishing the bunch in a bowl of cold water if it seems very gritty. Tear the leaves off the stems, roll them up, and feed into the juicer, pushing them through with firmer produce.
Chili peppers	Discard the stem. Wash and juice. Chilies are pretty spicy, so use with care. If you want a milder flavor, discard the seeds.
Chinese five-spice powder	Don't put this through the juicer—just sprinkle into your juice.
Cilantro	Wash thoroughly and juice both stems and leaves.
Cinnamon, ground	Don't put this through the juicer. Sprinkle it on juices, such as apple, pear, or sweet potato.
Coriander	see Cilantro
Dill	Rinse and pull the delicate fronds off the stem to juice them.
Garlic	The flavor is strong and so are the benefits—too many to list here, but trust me, garlic is a wonderfood. Use fresh garlic and peel before running through the juicer. Start with a small amount and taste your juice before adding more.

HERBS AND SPICES	HOW TO PREPARE
Ginger	Cut off the size you need for your juice. Then use a spoon to peel the skin off (I find this to be just as effective as using a knife). Ginger doesn't produce much juice, but it does add a distinctive flavor, so be careful not to go overboard.
Mint	Wash thoroughly and juice only the leaves. The flavor is great with grapes, pineapple, strawberries, and watermelon.
Parsley	Wash well, swishing the whole bunch in water if very gritty. Tear the leaves off the stems, roll them up, and feed into the juicer, pushing them through with firmer produce.
Tarragon	Gives a slight flavor of aniseed to vegetable juices. Wash and tear the leaves off their woody stems before juicing.

Substitution guide for juice ingredients

PRODUCE	ALTERNATIVES
Apples	Blackberries, cherries, grapes, honeydew melon, mango, peach, pear, pineapple
Arugula	Beet greens, chard, collard greens, dandelion greens, green cabbage, kale, parsley, spinach, spring greens, watercress
Asparagus	Broccoli stalks, green beans
Basil	Cilantro, mint, parsley
Beets	Golden beets, radishes, red cabbage, tomatoes
Beet greens	Collard greens, dandelion greens, kale, mustard greens, arugula, spinach, spring greens, watercress
Beetroot	see Beets and Beet greens
Blueberries	Blackberries, cherries, raspberries, strawberries
Broccoli florets	Cauliflower, green cabbage
Broccoli stalks	Asparagus, celery, cucumbers, cauliflower

PRODUCE	ALTERNATIVES
Butternut squash	*see* Squash, winter
Cabbage, green	Kale, red/purple cabbage, arugula, sweet green (bell) peppers, watercress
Cabbage, red/purple	Broccoli, cauliflower, green cabbage, radicchio, radishes, tomatoes
Cantaloupe melons	Honeydew melons, mangoes, papayas, peaches
Capsicum	*see* Sweet green/red/yellow (bell) peppers
Carrots	Butternut squash (pumpkin), parsnips, sweet potatoes
Celeriac	*see* Celery root
Celery	Cucumber,s jicama, zucchini
Celery root	Celery, jicama, kohlrabi, turnips
Chard	Beet greens, collard greens, green cabbage, kale, mustard greens, arugula, romaine lettuce, spinach, spring greens, watercress
Cherries	Blackberries, blueberries, raspberries, strawberries
Chili peppers (jalapeño)	Serrano peppers, sweet yellow or green (bell) peppers
Cilantro	Basil, mint, parsley
Collard greens	Beet greens, chard, green cabbage, kale, mustard greens, arugula, romaine lettuce, spinach, spring greens, watercress
Coriander	*see* Cilantro
Cos lettuce	*see* Romaine lettuce
Courgettes	*see* Zucchini
Cranberries	Blackberries, cherries, raspberries
Cucumbers	Celery, jicama, zucchini
Dandelion greens	Beet greens, collard greens, kale, mustard greens, spring greens
Fennel	Celery root, jicama, kohlrabi
Garlic	Shallots, scallions

PRODUCE	ALTERNATIVES
Ginger	Lemons, limes
Grapefruit	Blood oranges, clementines, oranges, star fruit, tangerines
Grapes	Apples, honeydew melon
Honeydew melons	Apples, cantaloupes, grapes
Jalapeños	see Chili peppers
Kai choi	see Mustard greens
Kale	Beet greens, chard, collard greens, green cabbage, mustard greens, arugula, spinach, spring greens, watercress
Kiwi fruit	Limes, mangoes, oranges, tangerines
Kumquats	Oranges
Leeks	Garlic, onions, shallots·
Lemons	Clementines, ginger, limes, oranges, tangerines
Limes	Clementines, ginger, lemons, oranges, tangerines
Mangoes	Kiwi fruit, oranges, papaya, pineapples
Mint	Basil, cilantro, ginger
Onions	Garlic, leeks, shallots
Oranges	Clementines, grapefruit, kiwi fruit, lemons, limes, mangoes, papaya, tangerines
Oregano	Sage
Parsley	Arugula, basil, cilantro, kale
Parsnips	Celery root, sweet potatoes, turnips, winter squash
Peaches	Apples, oranges, pears, plums
Pears	Apples, celery root, peaches, plums
Pineapples	Grapefruit, mangoes, oranges, pomegranates
Pomegranates	Cherries, pineapples, strawberries
Pumpkin	see Squash, winter

PRODUCE	ALTERNATIVES
Radishes	Beets, red/purple cabbage, sweet red (bell) peppers, tomatoes
Raspberries	Blackberries, blueberries, cherries, strawberries
Rocket	see Arugula
Rock melons	see Cantaloupe melons
Romaine lettuce	Butterhead lettuce, green or red leaf lettuce, radicchio
Scallions	Garlic, onions, shallots
Shallots	Garlic, onions, scallions
Silver beet	see Chard
Spinach	Beet greens, chard, collard greens, dandelion greens, kale, mustard greens, romaine lettuce, spring greens
Spring onions	see Scallions
Squash, summer	Cucumbers, zucchini
Squash, winter	Carrots, parsnips, sweet potatoes
Strawberries	Blackberries, cherries, raspberries
Sunflower sprouts	Broccoli, cauliflower
Sweet green (bell) peppers	Green cabbage, sweet red or yellow (bell) peppers
Sweet potatoes	Butternut squash, carrots, parsnips
Sweet red (bell) peppers	Radishes, sweet yellow or green (bell) peppers, tomatoes, watermelon
Sweet yellow (bell) peppers	Sweet green or red (bell) peppers, yellow tomatoes, pineapples
Tangerines	Grapefruit, lemons, oranges
Tomatoes	Radishes, red/purple cabbage, sweet red (bell) peppers, watermelon
Tuscan cabbage	see Kale
Watermelon	Cantaloupes, grapefruit, honeydew melons
Zucchini	Celery, cucumbers, summer squash

Let's talk about pulp

"I love juicing but hate wasting all that pulp!" This is a common complaint I hear about juicing. The good news is that there are plenty of uses for pulp. I asked our Reboot community what they do with it, and they came back with a whole book of ideas. Here are a few of my favorite ones. We've also included a selection of pulp recipes in the recipes chapter.

1. Make your own veggie broth (see page 203)!
2. Add to your favorite vegetarian burger recipe. It adds flavor, texture, moisture, and nutrition (see page 207).
3. Mix it in with your next smoothie for additional fiber.
4. Compost it and add it to your garden.
5. Make an Italian favorite, Spaghetti & Meatballs, into a nutrient-rich dish by using pulp to make Veggie Meatballs (see page 211).
6. If you don't have time to use the pulp immediately, place it in resealable bags and freeze it until you need it.
7. Feed it to your furry friends! Add a little leftover kale pulp to your dog's food bowl and watch your dog scarf it down. You can also make nutritious dog treats (see page 212).
8. If you have a hard time getting your kids to eat their vegetables, try adding the pulp to sauces, soups, and other dinner ingredients—they'll never know it's in there.
9. Make Banana, Carrot, and Zucchini (Courgette) Muffins (see page 205).
10. Raise your own chickens? Feed it to them!
11. Stir it right into your soups for added flavor and, of course, more nutrients.
12. Make gluten-free, raw Rosemary Carrot Flax Crackers (see page 209).
13. Use as a spread on sandwiches and crackers.

14. Add it to your favorite stir-fry or even omelet or frittata recipe.

15. Freeze the pulp after juicing ginger root and use it as a topical anesthetic for sore muscles and bruises.

16. Make a homemade face scrub. Anything from cucumbers, carrots, lemons, oranges, parsley, kale, radishes, etc., can be applied directly to your face. You can also mix in a bit of honey or oatmeal to help it stick.

17. Sprinkle it on a salad for added benefits.

18. Try it as an indoor plant fertilizer.

19. Use pulp from apples to make applesauce. Add a little ground cinnamon and a pinch of coconut sugar into a frying pan and warm until it reaches a nice consistency.

20. Enjoy it as its own salad. Think apple, carrot, and ginger pulp with chopped pineapple and coconut flakes!

21. If you have a dehydrator, dehydrate for a crunchy salad topping.

22. Mix leafy green pulp into your favorite healthy whole grain like brown rice, quinoa, and millet.

How to get the most nutritious, delicious produce

I'm asked quite often which juicer produces the most nutritious juice, but the truth is, there are multiple factors that affect the nutritional quality of your juice (and your food)—and it's not down to the juicer. The most important factor may be the actual produce. Not all tomatoes or cobs of corn are created equal. One of the twenty-first-century triumphs of agriculture is that we have been able to increase crop yields to feed an ever-expanding global population. But the cost of higher yields is decreased nutritional quality in the foods we are growing. Some studies show that today's produce contains 10–25 percent less iron, zinc, protein, calcium, vitamins, and other nutrients than historic crops.[3]

Other studies show that organic produce may actually be more nutritious than conventional produce. It seems that the pesticides and fertilizers that are meant to protect plants and create higher yields actually weaken their nutritional quality. A recent study found that organic tomatoes have double the amounts of anti-oxidants compared to conventional tomatoes.[4] And did you know that the more bitter fruits and vegetables often have higher concentrations of phytonutrients?[5]

There are other things that affect the nutritional density of all produce, whether it is high-yield, heirloom, conventional, sweet, or bitter, and that is exposure to oxygen, light, and heat. As soon as produce is picked, it starts to lose its nutritional quality. Why is that? Because as soon as it is picked, nutrients begin to oxidize into the air. The more extreme the light and heat exposure, the more rapid the nutrient loss. Leafy greens with a large surface area and no hard protective covering cannot be stored as long as other fruits and vegetables, and they lose their nutritional density relatively rapidly. Peels on citrus fruits and the rinds on melons protect their fruits from light and oxygen, which is why oranges and cantaloupes last longer if you don't cut them. Once food is exposed to oxygen, bacteria in the air also start to work, helping produce decay. Refrigerating food slows down the bacterial action, so it takes food longer to spoil. Freezing food stops the bacterial process (frozen bacteria are inactive), and some fruits and vegetables can be frozen up to a year without losing their nutritional density.

---

3   Brian Hallweil, "Still No Free Lunch: Nutrient Levels in U.S. Food Supply Eroded by Pursuit of High Yields," September 2007, *The Organic Center Critical Issue Report*, *http://organic-center.org/reportfiles/YieldsReport.pdf*

4   Aurelice B. Oliveira, Carlos F. H. Moura, Enéas Gomes-Fiho, Claudia A. Marco, Laurent Urban, and Maria Raquel A. Miranda, "The Impact of Organic Farming on Quality of Tomatoes Is Associated to Oxidative Stress during Fruit Development," February 20, 2013,
http://www.plosone.org/article/info%3Adoi%2F10.1371%2Fjournal.pone.0056354#pone.0056354-Foyer1

5   Jo Robinson, *Eating on the Wild Side: The Missing Link to Optimum Health. New York: Little Brown and Company, 2013.*

For some fruits and vegetables, the cooking process—heating food to 115°F/46°C or higher—can also decrease their nutritional density. Though this is not true for tomatoes; cooking tomatoes actually increases their concentration of lycopene, which has important cancer-fighting properties.

This is why I'm a fan of HPP bottled juices—HPP bottled juice is produced using high pressure, not heat, to pasteurize the juice, so less nutrients are lost in the bottling process. Making your own juice is still best, but HPP juices are a great option when you can't make your own. I know what you're thinking, "Joe, isn't a raw food diet best then?" Well I'm not someone who can live on raw food! While I eat a lot of raw foods, I also enjoy soups and vegetarian mains (and occasional ice cream and meat!). And I know that cooked fruits and veggies have an amazing amount of nutrition. For some fruits and vegetables, the cooking process actually increases the absorption of nutrients. That's why you can enjoy cooked vegetables during the eating portion of your Reboot.

What does this mean for you? The bottom line is, if you can, buy local (food is generally fresher if it hasn't traveled halfway across the world), look for heirloom varieties, buy organic, and use your produce as quickly as possible after you buy it—don't shove it in the fridge for a week. And know that frozen produce may not only be cheaper but might also be more nutritious than the same item out of season in the produce aisle. If you can't follow any of these suggestions, don't worry. I'll take conventionally grown carrots that were shipped across the country and then sat in my fridge for 7 days over 90 percent of the items on supermarket shelves.

As far as the most nutritious juicer? I don't think it matters much. There are no juicers on the market that heat up produce enough to kill nutrients. (My favorite, the Breville Juice Fountain Plus, heats up the produce one degree during the spinning process.) Use the juicer that works best for you and don't worry about which is most nutritious. Juice is nutritious—just juice on!

Juicing, blending, what's the difference?

They're both great, but they are *really* different, and it's important to understand why. When you blend, everything goes into a machine, you hit the "whiz" button, and then everything that went into the machine is poured out into your glass. You won't see the blueberries, chunks of apples, or kale leaves anymore . . . but they're all in the glass. It's the same calories and nutrition as eating them whole—just faster and more delicious.

When you juice, everything goes into the machine, but the liquid is separated from the solids. You will have a glass of juice and a separate container of pulp. If you don't have leftover pulp, you're not juicing. It provides almost three quarters of the nutrition as eating the ingredients whole does, but in a form that allows your body to quickly absorb the nutrients and gives your digestive system a break.

So which one is better? They're both great for you!

When you juice, you are removing the insoluble fiber but retaining 65 to 70 percent of the nutrients that are in the produce. And without fiber to slow down your digestion, your body rapidly absorbs the nutrients. Try eating 70 percent of the produce that goes into my Mean Green. And then do that five times a day. That's a lot of eating! That's why on a Reboot we recommend juicing. By juicing you are supercharging your body with nutrients. We've noticed weight loss tends to be faster when juicing, too. And after a lot of practice, I can tell you that there are some vegetables—beets, sweet potatoes, squash—that I think are just much better juiced.

When you blend, you are retaining the insoluble fiber. And yes, fiber is good for you. It helps maintain healthy bowels, lowers cholesterol levels, and slows the absorption of sugar—which is particularly important for diabetics. This is why our Reboot plans call for juices that are primarily made from vegetables (80 percent veggies to 20 percent fruit). They not only provide an important variety of nutrients but are also much lower in sugar. And if your post-Reboot diet is high in plant-based foods (which I hope it is!), you will be getting lots of fiber.

When I'm not Rebooting, I like both juices and smoothies. I will make a Mean Green juice almost every day, since it is such a delicious and efficient way to fuel my body. And sometimes I feel like having a Green Monkey with almond milk, bananas, and almond butter—ingredients you can't juice. (Web link for the recipe: www.rebootwithjoe.com/kale-banana-peanut-butter-smoothie)

SHOPPING AND COOKING

Produce shopping

When fruits and veggies become a bigger part of your life, so do trips to the farmers' market and grocery store. No more sitting in line at the drive-thru for your fast food! This means you have to spend more time preparing to shop, know what to look for while you are there, and learn the best way to store the beautiful fresh produce when you get home. Once you get the hang of it, it's all pretty simple. Follow these guidelines to make your next visit to the farmers' market or grocery store quick, easy, and affordable. Happy shopping!

BEFORE SHOPPING FOR PRODUCE

1. **Make your shopping list:** Go prepared with a detailed list so you know exactly what you need. This will not only will this make your trip faster but also help you avoid succumbing to any unhealthy temptations.

2. **Research seasonal produce:** Produce that's currently in season will be easier to find and will likely have the best price. Berries in the summer are half the price that they are in the winter.

3. **Eat a small snack at home:** Never go shopping for food when you are hungry. An empty stomach in the grocery store might lead to selecting unhealthy food choices.

4. **Bring reusable grocery bags:** Save paper and plastic by using your own bags. It's a great way to carry home (or to your car) your purchases versus ten plastic bags hanging from your arms, and it cuts down on waste.

5. **Bring the whole family:** Make it a family outing. It's a great opportunity to teach your children about healthy eating. They also make great shoppers when selecting new fruits and veggies to try!

1. **Bright is best:** Always select the fruits and vegetables that are brightest in color. If something is graying and discolored, it indicates spoiling. (Note: Avocados are the exception to this rule. Most bright green avocados are not ripe yet, so look for darker skin with a lightly firm touch.)

2. **No wrinkles:** Wrinkled, bruised, and cracked produce can indicate spoiling. This isn't always the case, though, and much of your produce can still be used, especially in a smoothie or a juice. But you be the judge—typically if it doesn't look like it should be used, don't buy it.

3. **In season:** Always try to shop in season! Seasonal produce is generally the cheapest and ripest product around. If you're shopping at a farmers' market, you'll likely have only seasonal options, so it will be easy.

4. **Fresh smell:** Our sense of smell can be the best indicator of freshness. If it smells bad, put it down.

5. **No bags:** We know this isn't always easy, but when possible don't buy any produce that is sold in plastic bags, unless it is coming directly from a farmer! And even when you pick up loose apples off the shelf in a grocery store, you don't need to put them in a plastic bag—just throw them right in your cart or your reusable grocery bag.

6. **Size matters:** Certain produce, like grapes and bananas, are often sold in plastic bags, but remember you don't always need to buy the whole bag! You can separate a bunch of bananas or a bundle of grapes and take only what you need.

7. **Dirt is your friend:** If the produce is fresh off the farm, it doesn't always look perfect. It may have a little dirt on it, it might not be perfectly shaped, but you will know it is fresh and nutrient-rich.

8. **The price is right:** Pay attention to the posted price. Is it per pound or per unit? If priced by unit, then go for the heaviest and biggest one you can

find! If priced by weight, then grabbing a smaller amount consistent with how much you plan to use will save you some money.

9. **Prioritize organic:** Prioritize and buy the organic items that are considered "The Dirty Dozen" by the Environmental Working Group in the US (listed on page 41). The Clean 15 do not contain as many pesticides, so if you are watching your wallet, you can skip these in the organic aisle.

10. **Frequent the frozen section:** Don't forget the freezer section, where frozen organic fruits and vegetables are always available. They last longer than fresh produce, are high in nutrients, and often go on sale.

Storing produce at home

1. **Determine the best location:** In the fridge or on the counter? If you do not know what produce you should refrigerate and what you should store at room temperature, notice how the grocery store stores it; if they keep something at room temperature, then so should you. If you're at the farmers' market, ask them!

2. **Know your fruits:** If storing in the fridge, place fruits in the produce drawer. Keep fruits that produce ethylene, such as apples, cantaloupe, honeydew melons, tomatoes, and bananas, away from other fruits and vegetables. Store fruits on the countertop with care. Keep fruits in large baskets or bowls on the countertop uncovered but away from sunlight and direct heat.

3. **Know your veggies:** When keeping fruits in the fridge, put them in the crisper to keep them fresh. Vegetables like onions, radishes, carrots, broccoli, cauliflower, leafy greens, and squash store best unwashed and in proper storage containers, like BPA-free produce savers. Store herbs by

cutting off the ends of the stalks and placing the bunch in a cup of water. Cover the top with a plastic bag.

4. **Wait to wash:** Don't rinse your fruits and vegetables prior to storing in the refrigerator. Washing these items adds water content, which will increase spoilage rates.

5. **Prevent spoiling:** If the produce you typically store at room temperature starts to brown or become softer, place it in the freezer or fridge! The colder temperature will slow the ripening process. You can also add them to a juice or smoothie immediately so they don't go to waste.

Washing produce

Unwashed fruit and vegetables can be contaminated with bacteria, so it is important to make washing your produce one of the first steps when preparing it for juicing or cooking. Both the National Health Institute in the UK and the Food and Drug Administration (FDA) in the US recommend washing all fruits and vegetables thoroughly in cold, purified water before juicing or eating them. If the water is purified, it helps you avoid harmful pollutants that are often present in tap water.

A few general tips for scrubbing: When washing cabbage or other members of the cruciferous vegetable family, like brussels sprouts, always remove the outer leaves first since they are generally the most contaminated. For leafy greens, first rinse them under cold running water and then place them in a bowl filled with water to get them really clean. Rinse berries and similar fragile fruits in a colander, while apples, pears, and other harder fruits can be scrubbed right under the tap. And don't neglect the produce with outer rinds and peels like pineapple, watermelon, mango, and citrus fruits! They need to be washed well, too, since contaminants on the outer skin may be transferred to the edible parts during peeling or cutting. Root vegetables with thicker skins like sweet potatoes and beets (beetroot) may be washed with a vegetable brush to remove potential bacteria.

If you are concerned about pesticides and/or food-borne bacteria, the following wash is a great natural disinfectant.

PRODUCE WASH

1 cup/8 fl oz/250 ml water
1 cup/8 fl oz/250 ml white vinegar
1 tablespoon bicarbonate of soda (baking soda)
½ lemon

1. Mix the ingredients in a large bowl to allow for the vigorous chemical reaction between the vinegar and bicarb (baking soda). When the reaction has stopped, pour into a spray bottle.
2. Spray your produce (you can use a scrubbing brush for firm items) and rinse well.

Organic, local, or conventional?

That's easy to answer—organic and local! But what if it's the middle of winter, you don't have organic options, or the organic ones are too expensive? I prefer local whenever possible. Local, seasonal produce is by far the best tasting, and shopping at a farmers' market allows me to support my community and gives me a direct connection with the person growing my produce.

The organic certification process can be costly and time-consuming; so many small-scale farmers may not be certified organic even though they are not using pesticides. The best way to find out is by asking! Get to know your local farmers; if you are buying directly from the growers, you can ask them how their produce is grown.

If you can't find a local option, then look for organic produce. But if organic is out of your budget, don't sweat it. The micronutrients in fruits and vegetables are full of disease-fighting properties. My preference is to eat fruits and vegetables. I prefer conventional to none!

If you can't afford to go completely organic and must be selective about what produce to buy organic, check out the US-based Environmental Working Group's list of the top 12 "dirty" fruits and vegetables (http://www.ewg.org/foodnews/summary.php), plus a few more. These are the ones to buy organic if you can. And remember—if you are eating conventional produce, peel before juicing or cooking.

DIRTY DOZEN PLUS

- Apples
- Celery
- Cherry tomatoes
- Cucumbers
- Grapes
- Hot peppers
- Kale (Tuscan greens)

- Nectarines (imported)
- Peaches
- Potatoes
- Spinach
- Strawberries
- Sweet bell peppers
- Collard greens

CLEAN FIFTEEN

- Asparagus
- Avocados
- Cabbage
- Cantaloupe
- Eggplant (aubergine)
- Grapefruit
- Kiwi
- Mangoes
- Mushrooms
- Onions
- Papayas
- Pineapples
- Sweet corn
- Sweet peas (frozen)
- Sweet potatoes (kumara)

LOCO FOR COCONUT OIL

You'll notice in most of our recipes that require cooking, we use coconut oil. Why? Coconut oil is very different from other common cooking oils, like canola and vegetable oils, because it contains a unique composition of 90 percent saturated fatty acids. This is what gave it such a bad rap for so long, but new studies that are emerging suggest quite the opposite.

Coconut oil is cholesterol-free and contains medium-chain triglycerides, or "good fats," and high amounts of lauric acid. The high levels of fatty acids make this oil very resistant to oxidation at high heats, making it ideal for cooking methods that require high temperatures. When oils are heated above their smoke point, like olive oil or flax oil, the oil becomes rancid, the chemical structure changes, and it produces blue smoke. Try to use olive oil for fresh salads so it doesn't need to be heated and you can reap its natural benefits.

If you don't like coconut oil, there are other high-quality oils that are excellent for cooking, like avocado oil and macadamia oil. Avocado oil is a great source of monounsaturated fatty acids and vitamin E and may even help boost absorption of carotenoids (a powerful antioxidant) and other nutrients. It naturally has an unusually high smoke point, which means it's good for cooking at medium to high temperatures. Macadamia oil is also among the more heat-stable oils and, like avocado oil, has a high percentage of monounsaturated fats, which may make it beneficial for heart health and anti-inflammation. It makes for a great oil to cook with at medium to high temperatures or to use raw on salads or in juices.

Coconut oil doesn't need to be refrigerated. Simply store it on the shelf. At a slightly cool room temperature, it may be solid, and on warmer days, liquid. Simply run it under hot water or pop it in the microwave if you need it in liquid form. You can sauté with it or use it in place of oil in almost any recipe. It's great for popping corn or as a butter substitute in recipes—try replacing butter with coconut oil in chocolate chip cookies. Sounds crazy, but it's delicious.

You can also use coconut oil in juices or smoothies. In fact, if you plan on Rebooting longer than 15 days, we recommend adding in 1 teaspoon of coconut oil to one of your juices during the day to help you maintain healthy levels of good-quality fats.

A–Z produce prep for cooking Reboot-friendly veggies

ACORN SQUASH

Looks like: An acorn-shaped squash that's got green and orange splashes; should feel firm to the touch with no soft spots.

Prep: Slice in half lengthwise, starting at the stem end, and scoop out the seeds and stringy bits in the middle.

Cook: *In the oven:* Preheat the oven to 350°F/180°C/gas 4. Place the two halves of the squash on a baking dish, cut side up, in about 1 in/2.5 cm water. Drizzle with coconut oil and sea salt, and bake for about 1 hour.

Note: You can eat the skins of acorn squash; when it's cooked well, it should have a similar texture to a baked potato skin. It goes great with a bit of maple syrup and cinnamon if you are craving a little more sweet than savory.

ARTICHOKE

Looks like: Tight green buds—watch out for browning or bruising.

Prep: Use kitchen scissors to snip tough outer leaves and trim the long bottom stem.

Cook: *On the stove:* Heat a bit of coconut oil in a large skillet; add the artichokes and stir for about a minute. Add 2 cups/16 fl oz/500 ml of water (or vegetable broth) and 1 teaspoon dried rosemary. Bring to a simmer; cover, reduce the heat, and cook for about 15 minutes. *On the grill:* Cut artichokes in half lengthwise and scoop out the choke (whiskers in the center). Toss with

1 tablespoon of coconut oil and ½ teaspoon sea salt. Preheat the grill, and then place the artichokes over a direct medium heat, turning once or twice, until soft to the touch, about 8–10 minutes. *Steam:* Put the artichokes in a large pot with about 2 in/5 cm of water and cook on the stove over high heat. Cover and steam until tender, about 15 minutes.

Quick tip: Buy frozen artichoke hearts for a quicker, prepared version of this veggie.

ARUGULA (ROCKET)

Looks like: A small lettuce with curly leaves; look for crisp, colorful leaves that are not wilted or yellow.

Prep: This green can be quite sandy, so give it a good rinse before using. You can fill a large bowl with cool water and swish the rocket around in the bowl, and all the grit will sink to the bottom.

Raw: Arugula is great in salads or as a substitute for lettuce in a wrap. It will add a peppery and sometimes spicy flavor.

Cook: You can also toss the leaves into a warm salad or pasta dish for an extra dash of green color and nutrition. It cooks very quickly, so add in the last few minutes of cooking.

ASPARAGUS

Looks like: Green spears; check for freshness by bending, as they should snap when bent.

Prep: Trim the stem ends and rinse.

Cook: *In the oven:* Preheat the oven to 400°F/200°C/gas 6 and spread the spears over a baking sheet in one layer. Coat with sea salt and coconut oil, and cook for about 10 minutes, turning once halfway through. *Steam:* You can quickly prepare asparagus by putting 2 in/5 cm of water in a pan and placing the asparagus in a steamer basket inside. Cover and steam for about 5 minutes—the spears should be crisp and bright green, just a little more tender. Season with sea salt, pepper, and a drizzle of extra virgin olive oil. *On the grill:* Make sure the grill rack is oiled, spread out the spears, and cook over a medium heat for about 5 minutes, turning occasionally.

AVOCADO

Looks like: A thick, deep-purple or black skin; should feel a little tender when you squeeze it.

Prep: Rinse and slice lengthwise around the pit. Then put down the knife and hold the avocado in your hands to twist the two halves apart. Remove the pit by scooping it out with a spoon, or leave it in if you are only eating half the avocado, as it will help to prevent the remaining flesh from browning.

Raw: You can easily spread it on sandwiches or veggie burgers by mashing it before you spread, or slice it into salads.

BEET (BEETROOT)

Looks like: A little dirty and rough-skinned on the outside, with a dark ruby or bright orange flesh.

Prep: Wash and peel off outer skin.

Raw: You can eat beet raw (especially in salad); simply use a veggie peeler to remove the tough outer skin and then shred the inner flesh into small pieces.

Cook: If you enjoy cooked beets, just give them a quick rinse (keep the skins on), add a little coconut oil and sea salt to the outside, wrap in tin foil, and bake in the oven at 400°F/200°C for 45 minutes–1 hour. Once done, the skin will easily fall off, and you have delicious beets that you can cut to your preferred size or shape. Try slicing them on top of a salad.

BELL PEPPER (CAPSICUM)

Looks like: Bright green, orange, red, or yellow bell shape; look for firm peppers with shiny skin.

Prep: Rinse and slice. Hold the pepper, stem up, and cut into quarters, removing the white pith and seeds from the center.

Raw: You can enjoy peppers in a salad; simply slice and dice as you like.

Cook: Peppers go great in a veggie chili or a pasta dish. *On the grill:* Put peppers on the grill until they are blackened, and then peel off the charred outer skin and enjoy the sweet roasted peppers on their own or with some fresh garlic and olive oil.

BOK CHOY

Looks like: A bunch of white stems and leafy green tops—watch out for any wilting or yellowing leaves.

Prep: Chop off the base of the plant to make it easier to rinse, and be sure to rub the stalks to remove any dirt or grit.

Raw: You can slice stalks and leaves and add into an Asian-inspired salad with fresh mint leaves and lime juice.

Cook: This hearty green goes great in stir-fries or as its own side dish—simply chop it and add to any stovetop dish. *Boil it:* Bring a pan of water to a boil and add the bok choy for about 2 minutes. Remove, and then toss in a little sesame oil, brown rice vinegar, and soy sauce.

BROCCOLI

Looks like: Little green trees; go for a high floret-to-stem ratio with no yellowing, should feel firm to the touch.

Prep: Rinse and chop off the florets. You can cut the stalks in half lengthwise and then into half-moons.

Raw: Chopped florets go great in salads or with hummus and other veggie dips.

Cook: Goes great in stir-fries and soups. *Steam:* Place stems in a steamer basket above 2 in/5 cm of water in a large pan on high heat. Cover and steam 2–3 minutes. Add the florets, cover, and leave to steam for another 5 minutes. Toss with fresh lemon juice, olive oil, and sea salt. *In the oven:* Preheat the oven to 400°F/200°C/gas 6. Spread the florets on a baking sheet in a single layer and coat with coconut oil and sea salt. Cook for about 10 minutes, turning once halfway through.

BRUSSELS SPROUTS

Looks like: Little cabbage heads; look for freshness by avoiding yellow or tattered leaves.

Prep: Rinse, remove any tough outer leaves, and trim the stem.

Cook: *Steam:* Place the sprouts in a steamer basket over 2 in/5 cm of water in a large pan on high heat. Cover and steam 5–7 minutes. *In the oven:* Preheat the oven to 400°F/200°C/gas 6. Cut the sprouts in half, spread on a baking sheet in a single layer, and coat with coconut oil and sea salt. Roast for about 20 minutes, turning once halfway through.

BUTTERNUT SQUASH

Looks like: A longer squash with a light orange skin.

Prep: Rinse and cut lengthwise, scoop out the seeds and stringy bits with a spoon.

Cook: *Steam:* Preheat the oven to 350°F/180°C/gas 4. Place the squash, cut side down, in a baking dish. Add ½ cup/4 fl oz/125 ml of water and then cover tightly with foil. Bake for 1 hour. Remove from the oven and let cool. Scoop out the squash and mash the flesh with coconut oil and sea salt. *In the oven:* Slice the butternut squash into half-moons, or dice it. Toss with coconut oil, honey, and cinnamon, and roast at 400°F/200°C/gas 6 for about 40 minutes.

Quick tip: You can find butternut squash already sliced in many supermarkets during the autumn, or canned and mashed.

CABBAGE

Looks like: Compact, round head of sturdy leaves—can be green or red, and the outer leaves should not be discolored or shriveled.

Prep: Remove the outer leaves and rinse. Cut the cabbage in half, slicing through the stem, and remove the core.

Raw: You can slice it thin, shred it with a knife, or use a food processor. It's a great base for a healthier coleslaw dressed with mustard and fresh orange juice rather than mayo.

Cook: Goes great in stir-fries, soups, and stews. *Steam/Boil:* Bring about 1 in/ 2.5 cm of water to the boil in a large pan, and add the cabbage wedges and salt. Simmer, covered, 8–10 minutes. Sprinkle the boiled cabbage with sea salt, pepper, and extra virgin olive oil to serve.

CARROT

Looks like: Firm, orange spear, preferably with greens at the end.

Prep: Cut off the greens; peel and rinse thoroughly.

Raw: Chop into bite-sized chunks for hummus and veggie dips. Carrot can be pureed into a carrot-ginger dressing for salads too.

Cook: Carrots are quite versatile in the kitchen, and they make a great base for almost any soup, stew, or sauce. *In the oven:* Preheat the oven to 400°F/200°C/ gas 6. Cut the carrots in half lengthwise and slice into half-moon pieces. Spread on a baking sheet in a single layer and coat with coconut oil. Roast for about 15 minutes. *On the stove:* Chop the carrots into half-moon pieces and sauté in a pan with a little coconut oil over medium heat for about 5 minutes. Season with sea salt and fresh parsley. *Steam:* Chop the carrots into smaller pieces and place over a large pot in a steamer basket set above 1 in/2.5 cm of water. Put on high heat, cover, and steam for 5 minutes.

CAULIFLOWER

Looks like: A head of little white trees; go for a high floret-to-stem ratio with no yellowing; they should feel firm to the touch.

Prep: Rinse and chop off the florets. Sometimes it's easiest to start by chopping the head in half and then into quarters.

Raw: Chopped florets go great with hummus and other veggie dips.

Cook: Goes great in stir-fries and soups. *Steam:* Place stems in a steamer basket above 2 in/5 cm of water in a large pan over high heat. Cover and steam 2–3 minutes. Add the florets, cover, and steam for another 5 minutes. Toss with fresh lemon juice, olive oil, and sea salt. *In the oven:* Preheat the oven to 400°F/200°C/gas 6. Spread the florets on a baking sheet in a single layer and coat with coconut oil and sea salt. Cook for about 15 minutes, turning once halfway through.

CELERIAC (CELERY ROOT)

Looks like: An unusual-looking, off-white, round root veggie.

Prep: Rinse and remove the base and top with a knife. To peel it, cut down the sides, close to the skin.

Raw: You can slice it thin into matchsticks or grate it coarsely and toss it into a salad.

Cook: *In the oven:* Make your own celery root chips. Simply slice the whole thing in half and then quarters, and slice each quarter as thin as you can. Toss the pieces in coconut oil, sprinkle with sea salt, and spread onto a baking sheet in one layer (may require 2 sheets). Roast the rounds at 350°F/180°C/gas 4 until they are golden brown, about 15–20 minutes. *On the stove:* Make a hearty soup by cubing celery root and mixing with potatoes, leeks, and veggie broth. Simmer ingredients on the stove for 30 minutes and then blend with a hand blender. Top puree with a drizzle of extra virgin olive oil and thin sliced scallions.

CELERY

Looks like: Long green stems, which should be firm and topped with fresh leaves.

Prep: Rinse and chop off the bottom stem.

Raw: Chop into bite-sized chunks for hummus and veggie dips. Goes great sliced thin and added to any kind of chopped salad.

Cook: Slice and use in veggie stir-fries, broths, or stews. *On the stove:* You can braise celery by simply adding slices to veggie broth in a saucepan and simmering on low 10–15 minutes.

Quick tip: Celery leaves are edible and delicious—use them in soups and stews.

CHARD

Looks like: Long stems with green tops; stem colors can be white, red, or yellow.

Prep: Chop off the base of the plant and separate the stems for washing. You can fill a large bowl with cool water and put a bunch of chard in the bowl—all the grit will sink to the bottom.

Raw: Roll the leaves into a cigar shape and slice thin. Toss into a salad with lemon and olive oil.

Cook: Chard is a mild-tasting green and goes well in stir-fries and pasta dishes. *On the stove:* Slice stems and leaves, and add the stems to the pan first with a bit of coconut oil or water. Cook 3–5 minutes, and then add the leaves and cook for another 5 minutes. Drizzle with olive oil, lemon juice, and sea salt.

COLLARD GREENS (SPRING GREENS)

Looks like: Short thick stalks and large, wide green leaves—watch out for yellowing leaves.

Prep: Wash these greens by plunging them into a cool bowl of water or gently rubbing them under a running faucet.

Raw: Collard greens work great as a substitute for bread. You can remove the stem and use the leaf to make a delicious veggie wrap. You can also lightly steam the leaves for a few minutes to soften them and take away the mild grassy flavor.

Cook: You can quickly chop the greens by stacking five leaves on top of each other and rolling them into a cigar. Then slice them into small strips. *On the stove:* Sauté the thin strips with vegetable broth, chopped garlic, and onion for about 10 minutes over medium heat. Serve hot as a side dish.

CORN

Looks like: Bright green outer husks; each ear should feel firm to the touch, and on the inside corn can be white, yellow, blue, red, or a variety of colors.

Prep: Pull back the husks and remove; rinse the ears.

Raw: Remove kernels from the cobs and add to a salad, or eat right off the cob.

Cook: Corn is great at a barbecue, whether it's on the grill or in a salad. *Grill:* Pull back the husks without removing them and pull out the silks. Soak the ears in water for 20 minutes. Place corn in husks over high heat and grill, turning occasionally, for about 5 minutes. *Steam:* Husk the corn and then cut the ears in half. Place the corn in 2 in/5 cm of water in a large pot on high heat. Cover and steam 4–5 minutes.

CUCUMBER

Looks like: A long green tube; some varieties are shorter (like Kirby) and others are longer (like English)—make sure they are firm to the touch.

Prep: Rinse and dry. You can peel cucumbers; if you are buying organic, eat the skin because it is good for you.

Raw: Slice, dice, or chop in any way and add to salads, or just enjoy cucumber slices with a little lime and paprika sprinkled over them.

DANDELION GREENS

Looks like: Arugula (rocket) but with longer, pointier leaves.

Prep: Wash dandelion greens by placing them in a large bowl with cool water and swishing the leaves around to remove the dirt. You can chop off the roots and stalks.

Raw: You can add dandelion to salads, but be warned it has a bitter flavor. You're better off cooking dandelion, if you're new to it. It does go well in a fresh pesto with basil, lemon, olive oil, and pumpkin seeds.

Cook: *On the stove:* Add a little coconut oil or veggie broth to a pan and sauté greens with chopped garlic for about 5 minutes.

EGGPLANT (AUBERGINE)

Looks like: A purple bulb with smooth skin, no wrinkles or soft spots.

Prep: Rinse and chop; you can keep the skin on or peel it. For most eggplant dishes, people don't use the skin. However, it is edible, so if you want to give it a try, you can eat it.

Cook: To help soften eggplant before cooking it, chop, generously cover with sea salt in a colander, and let it stand 5–10 minutes. Rinse off the sea salt before cooking. *On the stove:* Chop the eggplant into cubes, add to a warm skillet with coconut oil and fresh parsley, and cook for about 5 minutes. *In the oven:* Preheat the oven to 400°F/200°C/gas 6. Brush the eggplant slices with coconut oil and arrange on a baking sheet in a single layer. Cook for about 15 minutes, turning halfway through. *On the grill:* Brush the eggplant slices with coconut oil and place on medium heat for about 8 minutes, turning once.

FENNEL

Looks like: Small, white bulbs with green stalks and feathery fronds; smells like licorice.

Prep: Chop off the stalks and fronds at the point where they meet the bulb. Cut the bulb in half lengthwise and remove the core.

Raw: Slice thin and add to salads.

Cook: *On the stove:* Add sliced fennel pieces to a large pan with coconut oil or veggie broth, along with some dried rosemary and lemon juice. Let the mixture simmer for about 15 minutes, adding more broth as you need it. *In the oven:* Preheat the oven to 400°F/200°C/gas 6. Spread the fennel slices on a baking sheet in a single layer. Coat with coconut oil and cook for about 20 minutes.

GREEN BEANS

Looks like: Thin, firm green tubes with stems.

Prep: Rinse and snap off the stems with your hand.

Cook: *Steam:* Put beans in a steamer basket over about 1 in/2.5 cm of water in a large pan on high heat. Cover and steam for 5 minutes. *On the stove:* Heat a little coconut oil or vegetable broth in a large skillet. Add the beans and cook, stirring occasionally, for about 3 minutes. Add a squeeze of lemon and a handful of toasted almonds or pecans and serve warm.

JICAMA

Looks like: An oblong, white potato.

Prep: Scrub well to remove any dirt and peel. Jicama skin is not edible. You can grate the flesh or cut it into cubes or slices.

Raw: Jicama slices are delicious with a little lime and paprika or shredded into salads. It also goes great with hummus and veggie dips.

Cook: *On the stove:* You can easily sauté jicama cubes. Start with a little coconut oil or veggie broth, add sliced red onions, then jicama, and cook 5–7 minutes until tender.

KALE

Looks like: Long, dark-green, leafy bunches; some varieties have purple or red hues.

Prep: Rinse thoroughly under running water. You can easily separate the kale from its stem by holding it stem side up and pulling off the leaves with your hands. Then you can ribbon chop the kale by rolling it into a cigar shape and slicing it thin.

Raw: Goes great in salads. The trick is to massage the kale first with your hands and a little extra virgin olive oil. This helps break down the veggie, making it a little sweeter.

Cook: Kale is a great addition to stir-fries, soups, and sauces. *Steam:* To reduce its bitterness, simply add kale to a pan of boiling water for a minute or two and drain. Top with your favorite Reboot-friendly dressing. *On the stove:* Add a bunch of kale to a pan with veggie broth or water and simmer for about 15 minutes. Dress with olive oil, lemon, and sea salt.

LEEK

Looks like: Long, wide green stalks that are not bruised; should not be wrinkly.

Prep: Trim off the thick green leaves on top, leaving the pale green and white parts. Remove any damaged outer layers. Split in half lengthwise. Rinse under cold running water.

Cook: Leeks are a great substitute for onion in any dish. *On the stove:* Add chopped leeks to a large pan with veggie broth, garlic, and rosemary, and simmer for about 10 minutes. *On the grill:* Brush leeks with coconut oil and place on medium heat until lightly browned, about 5 minutes.

LETTUCE

Looks like: Big leafy greens; come in many varieties from romaine to bibb to green or red leaf.

Prep: Rinse thoroughly under running water and dry off either with a paper towel or in a salad spinner.

Raw: Romaine leaves are sturdy enough for a lettuce wrap filled with hummus or any veggie dip. Chop lettuce leaves to make a great salad with a Reboot-friendly dressing.

MUSHROOMS

Looks like: White, brown, or earth colored, cap or button shaped, with or without stems.

Prep: Use a damp paper towel or cloth to remove dirt from mushrooms; trim stems when needed.

Cook: Mushrooms go great in veggie stir-fries because they add a little extra moisture to the mix. *On the stove:* Heat a little coconut oil in pan over medium heat, and add sliced mushrooms and a pinch of sea salt. Cook 8–10 minutes, stirring occasionally.

ONION

Looks like: White, yellow, or red bulbs with flaky skin; be sure they don't have soft spots.

Prep: Trim off the stem end first. Remove the dry, papery skin with your hands; it can help to make a shallow cut down the side of the onion into the first layer and then peel. Leaving the root end intact, cut the onion lengthwise, cut the onion into quarters, and then slice, eventually removing the root.

Raw: Red onion can make for a pretty topping on a salad, or a little diced onion on a veggie burger always spices things up.

Cook: Add chopped onions to a pan as the base of almost any meal. *On the stove:* Add a little coconut oil or veggie broth to a pan on medium heat. Add the onions and sauté for 5 minutes.

PARSNIP

Looks like: A white carrot.

Prep: Trim the root and leaf and then scrub well.

Raw: Peel, chop up like a carrot, and serve with hummus or a veggie dip.

Cook: *In the oven:* Preheat the oven to 400°F/200°C/gas 6. Cut the parsnips in half lengthwise and slice into half-moon pieces. Spread on a baking sheet in a single layer and coat with coconut oil and sea salt. Roast for about 15 minutes. *On the stove:* Add chopped parsnips to a pan with a little coconut oil over medium heat and sauté for about 5 minutes. Season with sea salt and fresh parsley. *Steam:* Chop parsnips into smaller pieces and place in a steamer basket set above 1 in/2.5 cm of water in a large pot on high heat. Cover and steam for 5 minutes.

PUMPKIN

Looks like: A big orange ball with a stem. For cooking purposes, choose a smaller variety like sugar pumpkin.

Prep: Rinse and slice in half, starting from the stem and moving down. Scoop out the seeds and stringy bits. Rinse off the seeds and bake for homemade pumpkin seeds.

Cook: *In the oven:* Preheat oven to 350°F/180°C/gas 4. Place the pumpkin halves on a baking sheet or in a baking tin, add ½ in/1.5 cm of water, and bake uncovered for 1 hour. Remove from the oven and allow to cool. When cool, scoop out the insides to mash or use in any recipe that calls for pumpkin puree.

Quick tip: You can buy canned pumpkin—just be sure it doesn't have added sugars or preservatives.

RADISH

Looks like: Small red or white bulbs.

Prep: Rinse and remove the roots and leaves.

Raw: You can serve them whole, sliced, or diced with hummus or other veggie dips. You can grate them over a salad.

Cook: You can pickle them! For a quick recipe: Quarter 6 radishes, toss with sea salt in a bowl, and let stand for 30 minutes. Add 3 tablespoons of rice vinegar, 2 tablespoons of honey, and a piece of ginger (1 in/2.5 cm) to a saucepan over medium heat, stirring until the honey is dissolved. Transfer to a small bowl and leave to marinate for at least 2 hours.

SCALLIONS (SPRING ONIONS)

Looks like: Long green stems with small white bulbs at the end.

Prep: Be sure to rinse stems thoroughly and rinse inside the green part of the scallions.

Raw: Chop into small slices and scatter over soups and salads.

Cook: Add the green part of scallions near the end of preparation of a soup, such as miso, or add to stir-fry dishes for extra flavor.

SPAGHETTI SQUASH

Looks like: A large, yellow tube with a stem, usually about 12 in/30 cm long.

Prep: Give it a rinse and pierce it with a fork in several spots to prepare it for baking.

Cook: This squash works as a great alternative to pasta because the cooked squash easily shreds into thin spaghetti-like strands. *In the oven:* Place the whole squash in a baking tin and bake at 375°F/190°C/gas 5 for 1 hour. Let it cool for about 20 minutes, and then cut it in half lengthwise. Just like other squash, scoop out the seeds and stringy bits in the center. Using a fork, gently scrape around the edges of the squash and work toward the middle to create strands. Serve it with olive oil and sea salt, or top it with your favorite tomato sauce.

SPINACH

Looks like: Small, dark green leaves.

Prep: Rinse thoroughly under running water or fill a big bowl with cool water and swish spinach leaves around—any dirt will fall to the bottom.

Raw: Spinach salad is a classic!

Cook: Add spinach to any dish for a little extra color, but know that spinach cooks down a lot. If you're serving it as a side dish, use two to three times the amount you think you'll need. *On the stove:* Add leaves to a pan with a bit of coconut oil or water. Cook for about 3 minutes. Drizzle with olive oil and sea salt.

Quick tip: Buy ready-washed spinach in a bag and save the time of rinsing.

SPROUTS

Looks like: Small green leaves with long stems.

Prep: You can find anything from broccoli to alfalfa in sprout form. Rinse them thoroughly and enjoy on top of salads or in wraps.

SUGAR SNAP PEAS

Looks like: Fresh green pods with small peas inside and stems.

Prep: Rinse and snap off the stems with your hands.

Raw: Go great with hummus and other veggie dips.

Cook: Sugar snap peas are best in stir-fries. *On the stove:* Heat veggie broth in a pan over medium heat and cook for about 3 minutes. They will turn bright green.

SWEET POTATO

Looks like: A potato; should be very firm to the touch.

Prep: Scrub off any dirt. You can peel them, but then you will miss out on the nutrients and fiber.

Cook: *In the oven:* Make your own sweet potato fries! Preheat oven to 450°F/230°C/gas 8. Slice the potatoes into wedges, put them in a big bowl, and coat with coconut oil, sea salt, and chili powder, and then spread them on a baking sheet in one layer. Bake 20–25 minutes, occasionally turning them. *Steam:* Cut into pieces (1 in/2.5 cm) and place in a steamer basket set over 2 in/5 cm of water in a pan on high heat. Cover and steam for about 20 minutes. For mashed sweet potatoes, simply add almond milk and olive oil to the mixture.

Quick tip: You can find canned sweet potatoes, but just be sure they don't have added sugars or preservatives.

TOMATO

Looks like: A big red bulb; also comes in green, yellow, or striped; cherry tomatoes are the smaller, bite-sized version.

Prep: Wash and chop off the top with the stem, and then cut into slices. For a finer chop, keep going and slice and dice until you have cubes.

Raw: Tomatoes go great in salads, on top of a veggie burger, or diced in a fresh salsa.

Cook: You can use fresh tomatoes to make a pasta sauce or in veggie soup like minestrone. *In the oven:* Try slow-roasting tomatoes to get their full sweetness. Preheat the oven to 325°F/160°C/gas 3. Spread tomato slices on a baking sheet in a single layer, drizzle some coconut oil over the slices, and sprinkle them with sea salt. Cook for 2 hours—perfect for a day when you are home doing chores.

TURNIP

Looks like: Very firm bulb with red and white skins; can have greens attached at the top.

Prep: Rinse and chop off the root end and the greens. You can peel and then cut into slices.

Cook: *On the stove:* Cut the turnip into matchstick slices. Add a little coconut oil to a pan over medium heat, add the slices, and cook for about 10 minutes, stirring often. *In the oven:* Preheat the oven to 475°F/240°C/gas 9 and spread the turnip slices on a baking sheet in a single layer. Coat with coconut oil, sprinkle with sea salt, and cook for about 15 minutes.

ZUCCHINI (COURGETTE) AND SUMMER SQUASH

Looks like: A long green tube with a stem at the top; summer squash is yellow.

Prep: Wash and remove the stem.

Raw: Use a spiralizer to make raw zucchini noodles, or shred and toss into salads. (A spiralizer is a tool that is used to make long ribbons from vegetables; you can pick one up at a cooking store. If you can't get one, slice the zucchini in a food processor, with a mandoline, or use a sharp knife to make thin strips.)

Cook: This classic Italian veggie goes great in pasta dishes. *In the oven:* Slice into rounds and spread on a baking sheet in a single layer. Drizzle coconut oil and ground almond flour on top, and bake for 20 minutes. *On the grill:* Marinate in lemon juice, coconut oil, and garlic for at least 20 minutes, and then grill on medium heat for a few minutes on each side.

BASIC COOKING TECHNIQUES

- **Baking:** Place food in the oven, either on a baking sheet, in a covered or uncovered glass baking dish, or other oven-safe cookware, such as cast iron.

- **Barbecuing (Grilling):** With this technique, food is placed on a rack above a heat source. The process imparts a distinctive charred flavor. Avoid over-charring animal proteins, as this can create carcinogens.

- **Broiling:** This is done with heat applied from above. It is a great alternative to frying because it requires very little fat and gives food a crisp outside.

- **Roasting:** Similar to baking, but at higher temperatures. When roasting vegetables, line a baking sheet or roasting pan with baking parchment or aluminum foil to make clean-up easier.

- **Sautéing:** quickly cook food on the stovetop using very high heat and a small amount of fat (we like coconut oil) to brown the surface.

- **Steaming:** Use an electric steamer or a steaming basket over simmering liquid on the stovetop. It's best to steam vegetables lightly so that they maintain their color and crispness.

- **Stir-frying:** Heat a small amount of oil in a non-stick pan or wok on the stovetop. When hot, add small pieces of food (all roughly the same size) and stir rapidly with a wooden spoon or spatula. The aim is to cook food lightly and maintain its natural color and texture.

HOW TO PREPARE LEAFY GREENS

Leafy greens have many virtues. They are nutritional powerhouses packed with vitamins and antioxidants. They cook up relatively quickly and are pretty tasty too. Unfortunately, they are still one of the most missing ingredients in many people's diets. You may have seen them in a store in all their fresh, crispy glory but feel intimidated when it comes to knowing how to prepare them. Here's an easy guide to get you started.

- **In a juice:** Just rinse, soak in cold water to remove excess dirt and grit, and then push through your juicer's feeder tube and enjoy.

- **In a smoothie:** Add fresh chopped greens to your favorite smoothie recipe for a nutrient boost. Try banana, almond milk, frozen strawberries, and a handful of spinach or kale for a quick breakfast or afternoon snack.

- **In a salad:** For thin leafy greens like spinach, lightly toss them with your favorite dressing and top with nuts or seeds. I enjoy heartier greens like kale best when they are chopped in little pieces, stems removed, and massaged with a little olive oil or avocado oil for a silkier texture and a sweeter flavor.

- **In soups and stews:** Stir leafy greens into your favorite soup or stew to add a little green to the mix; try in a lentil soup or even in a heartier potato and leek version.

- **In a stir-fry:** Toss chopped greens such as bok choy, kale, or cabbage into a stir-fry and cook for an additional 5 minutes before serving.

- **Steam/boil:** You can retain more of your greens' brilliant color and more nutrients with a quick dunk in a large skillet. Here's how: Take about 2 cups/16 fl oz/500 ml of water for one bunch of greens. Bring the water to a boil first and add a little sea salt. Then add the washed, chopped greens and cook covered, on medium heat, 3–10 minutes, depending on the type of green you are cooking—as a general rule, the more bitter the flavor, the longer you should cook them. When you drain the greens, keep the water as a broth or just drink it.

- **Sauté:** Greens are great on the stove and cook up quick. Try chopped spinach, kale, chard, collards, or arugula in a pan with a little coconut oil, garlic, lemon juice, and sea salt. They cook up in 3–5 minutes for a great side dish. Raisins and pine nuts are great on top of greens and help complement the bitter flavor.

- **Bake/chips:** Kale chips are an amazing substitute for potato chips. Simply rinse the kale; tear into smaller pieces; and add coconut oil, sea salt, and paprika. Spread the kale on a baking sheet in a single layer and cook for 15 minutes at 350°F/180°C/gas 4.

- **What to do with chopped stems:** While you may be tempted to toss your green stems, consider adding them to an omelet or stir-fry, or simply sauté them in a pan with some coconut oil for a few minutes and then add them to your favorite dish.

FEEDING THE FAMILY WHILE REBOOTING

It's a bit ironic that many Rebooters are motivated by their kids to get healthy, but it is their kids that get in the way of a successful Reboot. If it's not facing the temptation of sitting down at the dinner table that you're the only one with the glass of liquid sunshine, then it's the extra work of preparing both dinner for them and juices for you. Here are some of the most helpful tips I've heard along the way from Rebooters all over the world:

1. If you're eating on your Reboot, let your family eat what you eat. Make enough of what you eat to feed the whole family but maybe add in a lean protein or whole grain to their dish. The recipes are selected carefully so that everyone can enjoy them, and you won't even miss the protein or the whole grains.

2. If you're just juicing, try incorporating the same fruits and veggies that you're drinking into dinner—you can juice sweet potatoes while the rest of the family has roast sweet potatoes.

3. Or, juice until dinner and then eat the cooked veggies while your family has additional grains and proteins.

4. When it's time to sit down at the dinner table, drink another juice while your family eats, and concentrate on drinking it slowly. You could even do the chewing motion with your teeth to slow down the pace.

5. Check out our pulp recipes for delicious ways you can use that leftover pulp. Your family will be getting so many added nutrients, and half the time they won't even notice. Carrots and beets are excellent for veggie burgers (see page 207)!

6. Have a juice on hand to enjoy while you are cooking to keep you full and keep your mind off all the smells that are coming out of your kitchen.

7. If being surrounded by your family's food is just too hard for you, ask your partner or your children to take over in the kitchen while you Reboot. Or find healthy takeaway options for them and drink your juice

alone while the family eats. It's OK if that's the only way you can say no to food!

Everyone is different, so just listen to yourself and find the way that helps you stay committed.

REBOOTING FOR THYROID CONDITIONS

A question often asked on our *Ask the Nutritionist* forum is "what fruits and vegetables should I avoid if I have a thyroid condition?" This is because it has been shown that some vegetables can interfere with the way thyroid hormones are manufactured by the thyroid gland.

Your thyroid is a butterfly-shaped gland that sits near your vocal cords and produces thyroid hormones that control your metabolism. Symptoms of an underactive thyroid gland include low body temperature, constipation, weight gain, hair loss, dry skin and nails, fluid retention, slow reflexes, fatigue, and slow thoughts and cognition. Thyroid problems can develop for a number of reasons, but the most common causes are deficiencies of nutrients such as iodine and selenium, autoimmune disease, genetics, stress, and environmental factors. The most common type of thyroid problem is hypothyroidism (underactive gland).

The concern for anyone with a thyroid issue who is Rebooting is that eating **raw** cruciferous vegetables can further suppress your thyroid hormone function and may also interfere with your body's ability to lose weight. So, if you have a thyroid issue, pay close attention to your veggies. Avoid consuming LARGE amounts of RAW cruciferous vegetables, including broccoli, cauliflower, brussels sprouts, bok choy, broccolini, Chinese cabbage, kale, kohlrabi, radishes, mustard greens, collard greens, choy sum, horseradish, and turnips.

This means you'll need to make some modifications to your juice—take my Mean Green, for example. Rather than including kale, substitute spinach or romaine instead and add more cucumbers, zucchini (courgette), or celery for that extra green. Cruciferous vegetables are certainly healthy and have been shown to support the liver in its natural detoxification processes, so if you are doing a juicing plus eating Reboot, have these vegetables cooked instead of raw. And eat them cooked when you've finished your Reboot!

It is important to note that if you have a normal thyroid function and consume adequate amounts of iodine, these vegetables will have no effect on your thyroid. Meaning that for anyone with a healthy thyroid, juicing lots of kale won't cause a thyroid problem. These modifications are only necessary for those with an existing condition.

If you have a thyroid condition, follow these healthy tips for a plant-based diet anytime, whether you are Rebooting or not:

1. **All fruits and vegetables** contain powerful phytonutrients that support a healthy immune system. Due to the inflammation seen in an autoimmune disease, it is important to reduce the inflammation with antioxidants by eating a rainbow of foods to provide valuable phytonutrients.

2. Eating **selenium**-rich foods such as Brazil nuts, shellfish, eggs, sunflower seeds, and garlic will help support a healthy metabolism. Selenium content varies in foods depending on the soil content—some geographical regions are very low in selemium. Selenium deficiency can be determined with a blood test, and otherwise by hair and nail analysis.

3. Healthy thyroid function also requires adequate levels of **iodine,** a trace mineral that is required by the body for the synthesis of thyroid hormones. Eat iodine-rich foods such as seaweed, marine fish, pineapple, iodized sea salt (avoid the free-flowing agent), spinach, and lettuce.

4. **Stress** can be a big factor that has a negative impact on your thyroid hormones and can fire up autoimmune activity. Commit yourself to stress-management techniques such as meditation, yoga, warm baths, exercise, reading, and other relaxing activities.

5. **Excess fluoride and bromide** exposure can interfere with the health of the thyroid. Fluoride and bromide can be taken into the thyroid gland in place of iodine.

6. **Avoid gluten if you are intolerant.** There are a number of studies that indicate autoimmune diseases, particularly Hashimoto's disease,

can be related to a gluten intolerance or celiac disease. You can find more information on gluten intolerance and celiac disease on RebootwithJoe.com.

7. **Avoid** sugar, caffeine, processed foods, preservatives, additives, and synthetic colors as much as possible.

8. **Coconut oil** has shown particular promise in some studies to help stimulate a sluggish thyroid.

So go ahead and feel empowered with a sluggish thyroid gland. With a few modifications to your Reboot, you can succeed in having excellent energy, health, and weight-loss goals.

REBOOTING FOR DIABETES

Diabetes is a disease where blood sugar levels are higher than normal or above a healthy range. The body produces the hormone insulin to move glucose/sugar into our cells. In diabetes sufferers, the body either doesn't produce enough insulin or can't use the insulin it makes well enough, so sugars build up in the blood.

The obesity epidemic, diabetes, insulin resistance, and prediabetes all go hand in hand. According to the US Centers for Disease Control and Prevention, 25.8 million people or 8.3 percent of Americans have diabetes. Seven million of these people are currently undiagnosed, meaning they don't even know they have this disease. As many as 35 percent of US adults over 20 years old and 50 percent of those over 65 have prediabetes—approximately 79 million Americans! Estimates suggest that at least 154,000 children and youth suffer from diabetes.[6] The Australian Government's Institute of Health and Welfare estimated that in 2012, there were 999,000 Australians with a diagnosis of diabetes, and over half the adult population was found to be overweight, putting them at risk of diabetes.[7]

The detrimental effects of diabetes are mind blowing. It is a major cause of heart disease and stroke, and it is the leading cause of kidney failure, lower limb amputations (non–trauma related), new cases of blindness, and the seventh leading cause of death. People with diabetes have twice the risk for depression, and depression itself can increase the risk of Type 2 diabetes by 60 percent. Diabetes can lead to complications with pregnancy, increased risk of infections, more difficult and complicated recovery from illness, and increased risk of dental diseases, and it also raises blood pressure and cholesterol levels. High levels of insulin in the blood or insulin resistance are being linked to increased risk for certain cancers and higher probability of cancer recurrence in survivors.

---

6   Centers for Disease Control and Prevention, "Diabetes Research and Statistics." http://www.cdc.gov/diabetes/consumer/research.htm
7   Australian Institute of Health and Welfare, "Diabetes." http://www.aihw.gov.au/diabetes/

The encouraging news is that up to 93 percent of diabetes cases may be preventable with a healthy lifestyle. And many Rebooters with diabetes have successfully participated in both juice-only and juice-plus-food, jump-starting into a healthy lifestyle and even decreasing and sometimes eliminating the need for medications.

But if you have diabetes it's important to customize your Reboot plan, taking certain factors into consideration, and to always consult with your doctor before starting a Reboot. For anyone with Type 1 diabetes or those taking insulin or other diabetes medications, it is especially important to discuss how to adjust your medication appropriately during your Reboot. (For more information see our advice on talking to your doctor: For Your Doctor, on page 215.)

If you have diabetes, we recommend modifying your Reboot.

- Consider the 10-Day Reboot plan or the first 5 days of the 15-Day Classic Reboot, which includes eating + juicing. The extra fiber from whole vegetables and fruits will help keep your blood sugar steady.

- Include blended vegetables/fruits. Fiber from complex carbohydrates in the form of whole foods is KEY. It will help keep your sugar levels steady and by making your smoothie or blend with mostly vegetables, you will also lower the total carbohydrate amount while keeping the nutrient levels high.

- Pay extra attention to hydration and drink plenty of water. When you're dehydrated, your blood is more concentrated and sugar levels can be higher.

- Stay active—exercise has its own way of helping keep blood sugar levels in check. While strength training is important, regular cardiovascular exercise has been shown to have the greatest positive impact on diabetic patients. See our Reboot Movement Method for ideas on healthy activities during your Reboot. Learn more about the Reboot Movement Method at www.rebootwithjoe.com/fitness.

- Create your juices with more veggies than fruits. Be sure to follow our tried and true 80/20 rule of 80 percent veggies and 20 percent fruits.

- Look for juice recipes that are listed as good for diabetes in this book; these are lower in sugar and carbohydrates.

And here are our top five tips for managing diabetes, whether on a Reboot or not:

1. **Eat small, frequent meals** throughout the day. Eating this way can help keep blood sugar levels stable and prevent overeating, which in turn promotes weight management. (Maintaining or working toward a healthy weight is so crucial for anyone with Type 2 diabetes.)

2. **Pair protein with carbohydrate-rich foods**, including fruits and starchy veggies. Protein- and fiber-rich foods are digested more slowly than carbohydrate-rich foods, making this combination key for keeping blood sugar levels stable and within a healthy range. Adding protein to carbs helps slow the absorption of sugar from the carbohydrate-rich foods. For example, almond butter on apple slices or a handful of almonds with an orange are good combinations.

3. **Eat a fruit or veggie with every meal and snack.** Increasing your intake of fruits and vegetables helps provide a healthy balance of nutrients like fiber, vitamins, minerals, and a wealth of phytonutrients. Eating whole fruits and vegetables helps control blood sugar. For example, it takes three whole oranges to raise your blood sugar to the same level as just 6 oz/180 ml of commercial, pasteurized orange juice. For fresh juices out of your juicer, we suggest more veggie-based juices.

4. **Drink plenty of water;** being dehydrated raises blood sugar levels by making your blood more concentrated. Hydration helps boost energy levels, reduces sugary cravings, and supports metabolism.

5. **Include cinnamon in your diet**. Research suggests that cinnamon can help keep blood sugar levels in check. Try sprinkling some into your favorite meals, including smoothies, fresh juice, and even chili!

AFTER YOUR REBOOT

When you have big health goals, you might need a drastic change in your diet to help you get there, and a Reboot is an excellent way to reset your system. It's what ultimately saved my life and set me up to remain on this path that has kept me 70 pounds lighter than when I started and, most importantly, medication free.

Sometimes I have to remind myself that I drank only fruit and vegetable juice for 60 days followed by 90 days of eating and juicing only fruits and vegetables. It still sounds pretty extreme, but my goals were extreme, and in the end I was able to achieve extreme results. At the end of that journey, I was able to look at myself in the mirror and recognize the person staring back at me—the energetic, athletic, healthy mate I once was—and I looked at my medicine cabinet and said, "Sayonara!"

While the benefits of a Reboot are countless, a Reboot is not a sustainable diet to maintain for the rest of your life. Our bodies need the right balance of protein, healthy fats, insoluble fiber, and a variety of plant-based foods to function properly over the long term. The beauty of a Reboot is that once it's done, you can still incorporate juices and heaps of fruits and vegetables throughout your daily life to maintain all the great benefits of a Reboot—clear skin, energy, weight loss, and health improvements—and continue to be in the driver's seat on the road to optimal health. But how to incorporate healthy proteins and fats and an occasional treat in your diet without backsliding into your old diet is where things can get a little tricky.

If you step into the diet and health section at a bookstore today, there are hundreds of different diets that promise you weight loss, health, and a fabulous physique. It's confusing to know which one to follow once you come off your Reboot. Well, let me tell you this. You don't need to follow one specific plan. You don't need to put a stamp on your eating habits by identifying yourself as raw, vegan, vegetarian, paleo, gluten-free, dairy-free, macrobiotic, pescatarian . . . I could go on and on.

However, if this helps you to stick to a diet that works for you, then by all means, go for it. I don't have a problem with any of these diets, nor do I endorse one over the other. It's up to you to determine what diet works for you. For me, a diet that is high in fruits and vegetables, along with fish and meat a few times a week and chocolate ice cream once every 7 to 10 days, works best. I stay away from gluten as I notice I tend to gain weight if I eat bread, and I have at least one juice pretty much daily.

When you come off of your Reboot, start adding in foods that you think are good for your lifestyle to find out what works for you. You may find that a diet filled with lots of plants, the occasional meats, and a grass-fed yogurt here or there is best for you. Or you may find it is easier for you to sustain your health gains by eating vegan. And what's best for you is the best diet out there. In the resource section, I've included a list of recipe books that have been inspirational and informative for Rebooters trying to determine their diet for life.

The recipes in this book are meant for Rebooting but are also excellent as part of an after-the-Reboot diet. They are a great way to continue consuming heaps of fruits and vegetables, and if you want to add something more, you can always incorporate wild fish, free-range organic chicken, grass-fed beef, or anything else you enjoy, such as quinoa or brown rice. There are also tons of plant-based recipes at RebootwithJoe.com.

DIETS DEFINED

Dairy-free: People following a dairy-free diet avoid anything with cow, sheep, or goat's milk products, including milk, cheese, and yogurt. Dairy is a common allergen. Many other diets are also dairy-free.

Gluten-free: A gluten-free diet (GF diet) is a diet that eliminates foods containing gluten, a protein composite found in wheat (including kamut and spelt), barley, rye, and triticale.

Macrobiotic: A macrobiotic regimen focuses on eating grains as the main staple, in addition to local vegetables, and avoiding highly processed or refined foods and most animal products.

Paleo: The paleo diet is an effort to eat like we used to back in the day. If a caveman couldn't eat it, neither can you. This means eating anything we would hunt or find, including meats, fish, nuts, leafy greens, regional veggies, and seeds.

Pescatarian: Similar to a vegetarian, but they include fish in their diet.

Raw: A raw diet contains only uncooked and unprocessed foods. People following a raw diet eat fruits, vegetables, nuts, and some grains.

Vegan: Vegans consume no animal flesh, including no red meat, poultry, or fish, or products that have come from an animal, such as eggs or any dairy product.

Vegetarian: Vegetarians consume no meat—including no red meat, poultry, or fish—but may include eggs and dairy products as part of their diet.

THE RECIPES

Please note the following general points, which apply to all the recipes.

- All the recipes use standard US/UK spoon measures: 1 teaspoon = 5 ml; 1 tablespoon = 15 ml. Note that in Australia 1 teaspoon = 5 ml, but 1 tablespoon = 20 ml, so take care when measuring. All spoonfuls should be level.

- A handful is equal to about 1 cup/8 oz/250 ml.

- All eggs and produce are medium in size, unless a recipe states otherwise.

- Wash all produce before juicing, blending, or cooking it.

- If you are unsure how to prepare a fruit or vegetable for juicing, check out our guide on page 16.

- Please note that the nutrition information for juices in particular is just an estimate. The actual calories and nutritional content will vary based on the size of your produce and the efficiency of your juicer.

- If using canned foods such as beans or tomatoes, some authorities (including the US Food and Drug Administration) advise against cans in which the inside is coated with Bisphenol-A (BPA), an industrial chemical that can transfer into food. The same goes for plastic storage containers and bottles made with this chemical. Some research studies have linked BPA to breast cancer and diabetes, as well as to hyperactivity, aggression, and depression in children.

KEY

Season: The ideal season in the Northern Hemisphere for one or more key items in the recipe, to help you get produce at its best.

Color: Try to drink a variety of colors. If substituting on a Reboot plan, substitute color for like color.

This is a quick and easy item to make, using few ingredients or elaborate preparation.

Great for post-workout—or if it's a juice, even during your workout.

Especially helpful if you have one or more of the listed health conditions.

Appropriate for a Reboot (which all the recipes in this book are, except for some of the pulp recipes).

JUICES

Autumn Harvest (Orange)

Autumn

R 🕐 🏃

+ Cancer, arthritis, gout, allergies, migraines, inflammation/pain, autoimmune conditions, thyroid, vision, skin, immunity

Nutrition per serving: 216 kCal; 906 kJ; 3 g protein; 49 g carbohydrates; 1 g fat; 0 g saturated fat; 0 g fiber; 18 g sugar; 58 mg sodium

1 butternut squash
1–2 red apples
1 tablespoon ground cinnamon
1 in/2.5 cm piece of fresh ginger root

Call for Fall (Orange)

Summer / Autumn

+ Heart disease, stroke, high cholesterol, allergies, migraines, thyroid, weight loss/obesity, vision, skin, immunity

Nutrition per serving: 172 kCal; 721 kJ; 3 g protein; 39 g carbohydrates; 1 g fat; 0 g saturated fat; 3 g fiber; 25 g sugar; 52 mg sodium

2 carrots
1½ apples
½ lemon
4 leaves romaine (cos) lettuce
5 strawberries

Celebration Grape Vino (Purple)

Summer / Autumn

R ⚕

Heart disease, cancer, arthritis, thyroid, GI, liver

Nutrition per serving: 248 kCal; 1,039 kJ; 7 g protein; 53 g carbohydrates; 1 g fat; 0 g saturated fat; 5 g fiber; 38 g sugar; 56 mg sodium

½ fennel bulb
½ head of red cabbage
2 large handfuls of grapes
1 green apple

Citrus Winter Warmer (Red)

Winter

+ Heart disease, stroke, high cholesterol, cancer, autoimmune conditions, thyroid, skin, immunity, GI, liver

Nutrition per serving: 232 kCal; 971 kJ; 5 g protein; 52 g carbohydrates; 1 g fat; 0 g saturated fat; 3 g fiber; 29 g sugar; 48 mg sodium

2 blood or regular oranges
½ ruby grapefruit
1 beet (beetroot)
1 sweet potato (kumara)
½ lemon
1 in/2.5 cm piece of fresh ginger root

Clean Green Bean (Green)

Summer

R

+ Stroke, diabetes, osteoporosis, thyroid, weight loss/obesity, skin, GI

Nutrition per serving: 123 kCal; 514 kJ; 5 g protein; 24 g carbohydrates; 1 g fat; 0 g saturated fat; 1 g fiber; 10 g sugar; 24 mg sodium

2 large handfuls of green beans (about 7 oz/200 g)
1 large handful of spinach leaves (about 7 oz/200 g)
2 cucumbers
1 lemon

Cooling Summer (Red)

Summer

✚ Thyroid, skin

Nutrition per serving: 239 kCal; 998 kJ; 5 g protein; 51 g carbohydrates; 2 g fat; 0 g saturated fat; 2 g fiber; 33 g sugar; 23 mg sodium

1 cup/14 oz/450 g strawberries
2 apples
2 zucchini (courgette)
2 celery sticks

Dark & Stormy (Purple)

Summer / Autumn

R 🚶

Heart disease, high cholesterol, diabetes, cancer, osteoporosis, arthritis, inflammation/pain, weight loss/obesity, immunity, GI, liver, menstrual/premenstrual syndrome (PMS)/menopause/polycystic ovary syndrome (PCOS)

Nutrition per serving: 121 kCal; 506 kJ; 6 g protein; 21 g carbohydrates; 1 g fat; 0 g saturated fat; 2 g fiber; 6 g sugar; 63 mg sodium

8 kale (Tuscan cabbage) leaves
1 large beet (beetroot)
1 bunch of fresh parsley
2 celery sticks
1 lemon

Deep Dive Green (Green)

Summer

+ Heart disease, diabetes, osteoporosis, vision, immunity, memory, liver, menstrual/PMS/menopause/PCOS

Nutrition per serving: 105 kCal; 441 kJ; 6 g protein; 18 g carbohydrates; 1 g fat; 0 g saturated fat; 1 g fiber; 6 g sugar; 66 mg sodium

4 kale (Tuscan cabbage) leaves
2 romaine (cos) leaves
1 small handful of spinach leaves
1 small handful of fresh parsley
4 celery sticks
½ cucumber
½ zucchini (courgette)
1 lime
1 in/2.5 cm piece of fresh ginger root

Divine Dreamsicle (Orange)

Autumn / Spring

R

Heart disease, stroke, high cholesterol, cancer, arthritis, allergies, migraines, inflammation/pain, autoimmune conditions, thyroid, vision, skin, immunity

---

Nutrition per serving: 237 kCal; 993 kJ; 5 g protein; 53 g carbohydrates; 1 g fat; 0 g saturated fat; 4 g fiber; 34 g sugar; 47 mg sodium

1 apple
¼ pineapple
1 sweet potato (kumara)
4–6 carrots

Extreme Green (Green)

Summer / Autumn

Heart disease, stroke, high cholesterol, cancer, osteoporosis, arthritis, inflammation/pain, vision, skin, immunity, liver

---

Nutrition per serving: 220 kCal; 919 kJ; 5 g protein; 47 g carbohydrates; 1 g fat; 0 g saturated fat; 1 g fiber; 32 g sugar; 13 mg sodium

½ cucumber
½ zucchini (courgette)
1 small handful of fresh parsley
4 kale (Tuscan cabbage) leaves
3 celery sticks
1 handful of green grapes
1 apple
¼ lime

Fall Back to Summer (Orange)

Summer / Autumn

➕ Stroke, cancer, arthritis, gout, allergies, migraines, inflammation/pain, autoimmune conditions, thyroid, vision, skin, immunity

---

Nutrition per serving: 222 kCal; 927 kJ; 3 g protein; 51 g carbohydrates; 1 g fat; 0 g saturated fat; 1 g fiber; 28 g sugar; 50 mg sodium

1 sweet potato (kumara)
½ cantaloupe (rock melon)
1 pear
Dash of ground cinnamon
1 in/2.5 cm piece of fresh ginger root

Fennel & Spice & Everything Nice (Red)

Summer / Autumn

Heart disease, stroke, high cholesterol, diabetes, cancer, osteoporosis, arthritis, gout, allergies, migraines, inflammation/pain, autoimmune conditions, weight loss/obesity, vision, skin, immunity, liver, menstrual/PMS/menopause/PCOS

Nutrition per serving: 213 kCal; 889 kJ; 7 g protein; 42 g carbohydrates; 2 g fat; 0 g saturated fat; 4 g fiber; 14 g sugar; 60 mg sodium

½ fennel bulb
4 medium carrots
2 red bell peppers (capsicum)
6–8 kale (Tuscan cabbage) leaves
2 in/5 cm piece of fresh ginger root

Field of Green Dreams (Green)

Summer / Autumn

R

+ Heart disease, stroke, cancer, osteoporosis, migraines, autoimmune
conditions, weight loss/obesity, vision, skin, immunity

Nutrition per serving: 146 kCal; 612 kJ; 4 g protein; 31 g carbohydrates; 1 g fat;
0 g saturated fat; 1 g fiber; 17 g sugar; 44 mg sodium

1 large handful of spinach leaves
1 cucumber
1 small handful of fresh parsley
1 apple
1 lime

Giant Green Peach (Orange)

Summer

R

+ Heart disease, stroke, diabetes, cancer, osteoporosis, arthritis, gout, allergies, migraines, inflammation/pain, autoimmune conditions, weight loss/obesity, vision, skin, immunity, liver, menstrual/PMS/menopause/PCOS

Nutrition per serving: 105 kCal; 438 kJ; 3 g protein; 21 g carbohydrates; 1 g fat; 0 g saturated fat; 2 g fiber; 12 g sugar; 55 mg sodium

1 peach
4 kale (Tuscan cabbage) leaves
2 carrots
1 in/2.5 cm piece of fresh ginger root

Heart Beet (Purple)

Summer / Autumn

R

+ Heart disease, stroke, high cholesterol, diabetes, cancer, osteoporosis, arthritis, gout, weight loss/obesity, vision, skin, immunity, GI, liver, menstrual/PMS/menopause/PCOS, gallbladder

---

Nutrition per serving: 248 kCal; 1,039 kJ; 7 g protein; 53 g carbohydrates; 1 g fat; 0 g saturated fat; 2 g fiber; 34 g sugar; 66 mg sodium

1 beet (beetroot)
2 rainbow chard (silver beet) leaves
2 celery sticks
1 broccoli stem
1 large handful of fresh basil
1 lemon
2 green apples

Heart Warmer (Purple)

Autumn

Heart disease, stroke, high cholesterol, cancer, allergies, migraines, vision, immunity, memory, GI, liver

---

Nutrition per serving: 232 kCal; 971 kJ; 4 g protein; 53 g carbohydrates; 1 g fat; 0 g saturated fat; 4 g fiber; 33 g sugar; 55 mg sodium

2 beets (beetroots) and their leaves
4 chard (silver beet) leaves
2 carrots
2 apples
1 in/2.5 cm piece of fresh ginger root

Heartbreak Hill (Red)

Autumn / Winter

R 🏃

✚ Heart disease, stroke, high cholesterol, arthritis, inflammation/pain,
thyroid, immunity, GI, liver

Nutrition per serving: 157 kCal; 655 kJ; 4 g protein; 34 g carbohydrates; 1 g fat;
0 g saturated fat; 5 g fiber; 24 g sugar; 34 mg sodium

2 small beets (beetroots)

2 oranges

2 romaine (cos) lettuce leaves

2 in/5 cm slice of fresh ginger root

Heavenly Honeydew (Green)

Summer

R

+ Diabetes, osteoporosis, thyroid, weight loss/obesity, skin, menstrual/
PMS/menopause/PCOS

Nutrition per serving: 98 kCal; 408 kJ; 3 g protein; 19 g carbohydrates; 1 g fat;
0 g saturated fat; 1 g fiber; 11 g sugar; 64 mg sodium

1 handful of spinach leaves
¼ honeydew melon
1 cucumber
1 lemon

Holly Jolly (Green)

Winter

R

✚ Heart disease, stroke, cancer, inflammation/pain, immunity, memory, GI, liver

---

Nutrition per serving: 249 kCal; 1,042 kJ; 7 g protein; 51 g carbohydrates; 2 g fat; 0 g saturated fat; 5 g fiber; 36 g sugar; 51 mg sodium

¼ head of red cabbage

5 small or 2 medium beets (beetroots)

3 clementines or 1 orange

½ cup/115 g pomegranate seeds

2 large romaine (cos) lettuce leaves

Joe's Mean Green (Green)

Summer / Autumn

+ Heart disease, high cholesterol, cancer, osteoporosis, arthritis, migraines, inflammation/pain, autoimmune conditions, weight loss/obesity, vision, skin, immunity, liver

---

Nutrition per serving: 251 kCal; 1,049 kJ; 6 g protein; 54 g carbohydrates; 1 g fat; 0 g saturated fat; 2 g fiber; 30 g sugar; 128 mg sodium

8 kale (Tuscan cabbage) leaves
1 cucumber
4 celery sticks
2 apples
½ lemon
1 in/2.5 cm piece of fresh ginger root

Joyous Julius (Orange)

Autumn

+ Heart disease, stroke, high cholesterol, cancer, arthritis, allergies, migraines, inflammation/pain, autoimmune conditions, thyroid, vision, skin, immunity

Nutrition per serving: 159 kCal; 666 kJ; 4 g protein; 34 g carbohydrates; 1 g fat; 0 g saturated fat; 4 g fiber; 21 g sugar; 59 mg sodium

1 orange bell pepper (capsicum)

1 orange

5 carrots

1 large handful of spinach leaves

Kumquat Kooler (Orange)

Winter

+ Heart disease, stroke, cancer, arthritis, gout, allergies, inflammation/
pain, thyroid, vision, skin, immunity

Nutrition per serving: 181 kCal; 756 kJ; 4 g protein; 38 g carbohydrates; 1 g fat;
0 g saturated fat; 4 g fiber; 20 g sugar; 59 mg sodium

6 kumquats
1 orange bell pepper (capsicum)
8 carrots
1 in/2.5 cm piece of fresh ginger root

Lean Green Pineapple (Green)

Spring

✚ Heart disease, diabetes, cancer, osteoporosis, arthritis, gout, inflammation/pain, autoimmune conditions, thyroid

---

Nutrition per serving: 160 kCal; 669 kJ; 7 g protein; 31 g carbohydrates; 1 g fat; 0 g saturated fat; 1 g fiber; 16 g sugar; 55 mg sodium

2 large handfuls of spinach leaves (about 12 oz/340 g)
¼ pineapple
1 lemon

Lime Dance (Green)

Spring

+ Diabetes, osteoporosis, migraines, inflammation/pain, weight loss/ obesity, vision, skin, immunity, GI, liver, menstrual/PMS/menopause/ PCOS

Nutrition per serving: 157 kCal; 655 kJ; 3 g protein; 34 g carbohydrates; 1 g fat; 0 g saturated fat; 4 g fiber; 19 g sugar; 50 mg sodium

¼ pineapple

1 cucumber

1 lime

1 handful of fresh cilantro (coriander)

1 large handful of dandelion greens

Morning "OJ" (left), see page 116, and Heartbreak Hill, see page 105.

Sweet Mango, Avocado, and Tomato Salad, see page 171.

Raz Avocado Smoothie, see page 157.

Sweet Bunny Love Smoothie, see page 159.

Pear and Roasted Brussels Sprouts, see page 191.

Fresh Fennel and Avocado Salad, see page 166.

Spicy Roots Soup, see page 180.

Caprese Kale Sauté, see page 185.

Sweet Potato Sliders,
see page 196.

Colorful Cold Weather Salad, see page 164.

Baked Zucchini with Herbs, see page 193.

Summertime Watermelon Gazpacho,
see page 182.

Roasted Carrots & Avocado Salad, see page 170.

Watermelon Mint Salad, see page 172.

Zucchini (Courgette) Noodles with Fresh &
Easy Herb Tomato Sauce, see page 200.

Heavenly Honeydew (left), see page 106,
and Lean Green Pineapple, see page 111.

Love Your Broccoli (Orange)

Summer / Autumn

Stroke, cancer, allergies, migraines, vision, skin, immunity

Nutrition per serving: 120 kCal; 503 kJ; 5 g protein; 24 g carbohydrates; 1 g fat; 0 g saturated fat; 3 g fiber; 11 g sugar; 60 mg sodium

4 carrots
6 strawberries
1 broccoli stem

Lucky Leprechaun (Red)

Summer / Autumn

Diabetes, cancer, allergies, migraines, autoimmune conditions, weight loss/obesity, vision, skin, immunity, GI, liver, menstrual/PMS/menopause/PCOS, gallbladder

---

Nutrition per serving: 233 kCal; 976 kJ; 8 g protein; 46 g carbohydrates; 2 g fat; 0 g saturated fat; 4 g fiber; 16 g sugar; 45 mg sodium

5 medium–large carrots
1 medium tomato
½ head of broccoli
1 handful of fresh parsley
1 lime
2 in/5 cm piece of fresh ginger root

Mint to Be Green (Green)

Summer

R

Heart disease, diabetes, arthritis, inflammation/pain, thyroid, weight loss/obesity, skin, menstrual/PMS/menopause/PCOS

Nutrition per serving: 100 kCal; 419 kJ; 3 g protein; 20 g carbohydrates; 1 g fat; 0 g saturated fat; 0 g fiber; 9 g sugar; 34 mg sodium

¼ honeydew melon
2 celery sticks
½ cucumber
½ lime
1 handful of fresh mint

Morning "OJ" (Orange)

Summer / Autumn

+ Stroke, diabetes, cancer, arthritis, allergies, migraines, inflammation/
pain, autoimmune conditions, thyroid, weight loss/obesity, vision, skin,
immunity, menstrual/PMS/menopause/PCOS

Nutrition per serving: 118 kCal; 492 kJ; 3 g protein; 25 g carbohydrates; 1 g fat;
0 g saturated fat; 2 g fiber; 10 g sugar; 51 mg sodium

1 orange bell pepper (capsicum)
1 yellow bell pepper (capsicum)
1 large carrot
½ green apple
½ lemon

Morning Red Riser (Red)

Summer / Autumn

R 🏃

➕ Cancer, migraines, thyroid, vision, skin, immunity, GI

Nutrition per serving: 184 kCal; 770 kJ; 4 g protein; 38 g carbohydrates; 2 g fat; 0 g saturated fat; 2 g fiber; 28 g sugar; 51 mg sodium

1 beet (beetroot)
1 purple carrot (or orange carrot)
12 strawberries
2 oranges
2 celery sticks

New Beginnings (Purple)

Summer / Autumn

R ⫞

✚ Stroke, thyroid, vision, skin, immunity, GI, liver

Nutrition per serving: 183 kCal; 767 kJ; 5 g protein; 38 g carbohydrates; 1 g fat; 0 g saturated fat; 4 g fiber; 22 g sugar; 64 mg sodium

4 large carrots
2 medium beets (beetroots)
2 medium red bell peppers (capsicum)
1 in/2.5 cm piece of fresh ginger root

Not Too Sweet Cucumber Melon (Green)

Summary

➕ Heart disease, diabetes, autoimmune conditions, thyroid, weight loss/
obesity, skin, menstrual/PMS/menopause/PCOS

Nutrition per serving: 118 kCal; 492 kJ; 4 g protein; 24 g carbohydrates; 1 g fat;
0 g saturated fat; 0 g fiber; 14 g sugar; 38 mg sodium

2 large cucumbers
¼ honeydew melon
3 celery sticks

Passionate Plum (Green)

Summer / Autumn

+ Heart disease, arthritis, thyroid, weight loss/obesity, skin, memory

Nutrition per serving: 98 kCal; 411 kJ; 2 g protein; 18 g carbohydrates; 2 g fat; 0 g saturated fat; 1 g fiber; 14 g sugar; 50 mg sodium

1 cucumber
5 celery sticks
1–2 plums

Picnic Party (Green)

Summer

R 🏃

➕ Arthritis, gout, allergies, immunity, GI, liver

Nutrition per serving: 222 kCal; 930 kJ; 7 g protein; 46 g carbohydrates; 1 g fat; 0 g saturated fat; 5 g fiber; 26 g sugar; 50 mg sodium

1 yellow beet (beetroot)
½ grapefruit
1 summer squash
½ cucumber
¼ head of green cabbage
1 apple (or pear)
1 small handful of fresh mint

Pineapple Power (Green)

Spring

+ Heart disease, stroke, high cholesterol, diabetes, cancer, osteoporosis, arthritis, migraines, inflammation/pain, weight loss/obesity, vision, skin, immunity, GI, liver, menstrual/PMS/menopause/PCOS, gallbladder

Nutrition per serving: 133 kCal; 558 kJ; 4 g protein; 28 g carbohydrates; 1 g fat; 0 g saturated fat; 1 g fiber; 16 g sugar; 51 mg sodium

¼ pineapple
1 large handful of watercress
4–6 kale (Tuscan cabbage) leaves
2 celery sticks

Pink Lemonade (Red)

Summer

R

+ Stroke, cancer, inflammation/pain, autoimmune conditions, skin, immunity, GI, liver, gallbladder

Nutrition per serving: 241 kCal; 1,006 kJ; 7 g protein; 51 g carbohydrates; 1 g fat; 0 g saturated fat; 4 g fiber; 29 g sugar; 52 mg sodium

2 pears
1 lemon
¼ head of green cabbage
1 large handful of spinach leaves
1 small handful of fresh mint
12 strawberries

Piping Hot Pepper (Red)

Summary / Autumn

Heart disease, stroke, high cholesterol, diabetes, cancer, arthritis, inflammation/pain, autoimmune conditions, thyroid, weight loss/obesity, vision, skin, immunity, GI, menstrual/PMS/menopause/PCOS

Nutrition per serving: 105 kCal; 438 kJ; 3 g protein; 21 g carbohydrates; 1 g fat; 0 g saturated fat; 1 g fiber; 10 g sugar; 44 mg sodium

1 green pepper (capsicum)

1 yellow pepper (capsicum)

1 red pepper (capsicum)

1 chili pepper (optional)

2 celery sticks

1 lime

1 small handful of fresh cilantro (coriander)

Purest Green (Green)

Winter

R

✚ Heart disease, osteoporosis, weight loss/obesity, skin, immunity, memory, GI, gallbladder

---

Nutrition per serving: 209 kCal; 876 kJ; 8 g protein; 42 g carbohydrates; 1 g fat; 0 g saturated fat; 4 g fiber; 14 g sugar; 52 mg sodium

8 kale (Tuscan cabbage) leaves

1 cucumber

¼ head of cabbage

4 celery sticks

1 orange

1 lime

Rainbow Bright (Green)

Autumn

+ Heart disease, stroke, high cholesterol, osteoporosis, allergies, migraines, autoimmune conditions, vision, skin, immunity, liver

---

Nutrition per serving: 241 kCal; 1,006 kJ; 4 g protein; 53 g carbohydrates; 1 g fat; 0 g saturated fat; 4 g fiber; 33 g sugar; 54 mg sodium

4 kale (Tuscan cabbage) leaves
3 celery sticks
4 carrots
2 apples

Skin Brightening (Green)

Autumn / Winter

R ⏱

✚ Heart disease, cancer, osteoporosis, allergies, migraines, skin, weight loss/obesity, immunity, GI, liver, gallbladder

---

Nutrition per serving: 265 kCal; 1,107 kJ; 10 g protein; 52 g carbohydrates; 2 g fat; 0 g saturated fat; 5 g fiber; 27 g sugar; 64 mg sodium

2 oranges
2 carrots
1 head of broccoli
2 celery sticks

Slim Grin (Green)

Autumn

+ Heart disease, migraines, thyroid, skin, immunity

Nutrition per serving: 245 kCal; 1,025 kJ; 3 g protein; 57 g carbohydrates; 1 g fat; 0 g saturated fat; 2 g fiber; 35 g sugar; 64 mg sodium

2 large green pears
1 handful of green grapes
1 large bunch of spinach leaves
1 cucumber

Spiced Sweet Potato (Orange)

Winter

+ Stroke, cancer, allergies, migraines, autoimmune conditions, thyroid, vision, skin, immunity

---

Nutrition per serving: 146 kCal; 612 kJ; 3 g protein; 33 g carbohydrates; 1 g fat; 0 g saturated fat; 2 g fiber; 14 g sugar; 49 mg sodium

1 large sweet potato (kumara)

2 carrots

1 tangerine

¼ teaspoon ground cinnamon

Dash of nutmeg

Springing High (Green)

Autumn

Heart disease, cancer, osteoporosis, arthritis, gout, migraines, inflammation/pain, autoimmune conditions, weight loss/obesity, vision, skin, immunity, liver

---

Nutrition per serving: 241 kCal; 1,006 kJ; 5 g protein; 52 g carbohydrates; 1 g fat; 0 g saturated fat; 2 g fiber; 26 g sugar; 53 mg sodium

1 fennel bulb
6 kale (Tuscan cabbage) leaves
2 limes
2 apples

Summer Shine (Orange)

Summer

R 🏃

➕ Heart disease, cancer, allergies, autoimmune conditions, thyroid, vision, skin

---

Nutrition per serving: 118 kCal; 495 kJ; 3 g protein; 25 g carbohydrates; 1 g fat; 0 g saturated fat; 2 g fiber; 16 g sugar; 104 mg sodium

5 celery sticks
½ cucumber
1 large carrot
1 tomato
½ orange
½ peach

Sunny Green (Green)

Spring

R 🏃

➕ Diabetes, inflammation/pain, thyroid, weight loss/obesity, skin

---

Nutrition per serving: 207 kCal; 868 kJ; 7 g protein; 41 g carbohydrates; 2 g fat; 0 g saturated fat; 1 g fiber; 22 g sugar; 72 mg sodium

¼ pineapple
4 celery sticks
1 large bunch of romaine (cos) lettuce
1 handful of spinach leaves
1 lime

Sunny Pineapple (Yellow)

Spring

✚ Arthritis, gout, migraines, inflammation/pain, autoimmune conditions, thyroid, skin

---

Nutrition per serving: 107 kCal; 449 kJ; 2 g protein; 23 g carbohydrates; 1 g fat; 0 g saturated fat; 1 g fiber; 16 g sugar; 46 mg sodium

¼ pineapple
4 celery sticks
1 in/2.5 cm piece of fresh ginger root

Sweet & Sour (Green)

Winter

R ⏲ 🏃

✚ Osteoporosis, arthritis, gout, thyroid, skin, immunity

Nutrition per serving: 138 kCal; 579 kJ; 3 g protein; 30 g carbohydrates; 1 g fat; 0 g saturated fat; 4 g fiber; 24 g sugar; 54 mg sodium

2 large handfuls of spinach leaves (about 12 oz/340 g)
3 celery sticks
2 grapefruits

Sweet 'N' Tangy (Green)

Summer / Autumn

Heart disease, high cholesterol, cancer, osteoporosis, arthritis, inflammation/pain, weight loss/obesity, skin, liver

---

Nutrition per serving: 196 kCal; 819 kJ; 3 g protein; 44 g carbohydrates; 1 g fat; 0 g saturated fat; 2 g fiber; 23 g sugar; 68 mg sodium

1 large radish
1 small apple
1 pear
½ fennel bulb
4 kale (Tuscan cabbage) leaves

Sweet Sage (Green)

Autumn / Winter

+ Heart disease, stroke, high cholesterol, inflammation/pain, autoimmune conditions, weight loss/obesity, liver

---

Nutrition per serving: 155 kCal; 647 kJ; 3 g protein; 33 g carbohydrates; 1 g fat; 0 g saturated fat; 4 g fiber; 12 g sugar; 57 mg sodium

½ lime
1 handful of fresh sage leaves
2 celery sticks
1–2 pears
¼ head of green cabbage

Trick-or-Treat (Orange)

Autumn

R

Heart disease, stroke, high cholesterol, diabetes, cancer, arthritis, gout, allergies, migraines, inflammation/pain, thyroid, vision, skin, immunity, menstrual/PMS/menopause/PCOS

Nutrition per serving: 162 kCal; 677 kJ; 3 g protein; 36 g carbohydrates; 1 g fat; 0 g saturated fat; 3 g fiber; 16 g sugar; 57 mg sodium

1 sweet potato (kumara)

1 orange

1 orange bell pepper (capsicum)

1 carrot

Dash of ground cinnamon

Tropical Mint (Yellow)

Spring

R ⏲ ⚹

 Arthritis, gout, inflammation/pain, autoimmune conditions, thyroid, skin

Nutrition per serving: 219 kCal; 917 kJ; 4 g protein; 49 g carbohydrates; 1 g fat; 0 g saturated fat; 0 g fiber; 33 g sugar; 13 mg sodium

½ pineapple
1 cucumber
1 large handful of fresh mint
1 in/2.5 cm piece of fresh ginger root

Turnip the Greens (Green)

Autumn

R

+ Heart disease, migraines, autoimmune conditions, thyroid, weight loss/
obesity, vision, skin, immunity

Nutrition per serving: 180 kCal; 753 kJ; 4 g protein; 40 g carbohydrates; 1 g fat;
0 g saturated fat; 3 g fiber; 25 g sugar; 64 mg sodium

1 large turnip

1 pear

½ cucumber

2 handfuls of spinach leaves

¼ cantaloupe (rock melon)

1 large carrot

Warrior Princess (Red)

Summer / Autumn

R 🏃

Heart disease, stroke, high cholesterol, cancer, inflammation/pain, vision, skin, immunity, GI, liver

Nutrition per serving: 227 kCal; 949 kJ; 6 g protein; 49 g carbohydrates; 1 g fat; 0 g saturated fat; 5 g fiber; 33 g sugar; 58 mg sodium

½ head of red cabbage
½ small watermelon
2 oranges
½ fennel bulb

Watercress Wonder (Green)

Spring

R ⏰ 🏃

✚ Heart disease, high cholesterol, cancer, arthritis, skin, liver, gallbladder

---

Nutrition per serving: 167 kCal; 699 kJ; 1 g protein; 39 g carbohydrates; 1 g fat; 0 g saturated fat; 1 g fiber; 26 g sugar; 46 mg sodium

1 large bunch of watercress (7 oz/200 g)
2 green apples
1 lime
2 celery sticks

Workout to the Beet (Purple)

Autumn / Winter

+ Heart disease, stroke, cancer, thyroid, weight loss/obesity, skin, memory, GI

Nutrition per serving: 201 kCal; 840 kJ; 6 g protein; 43 g carbohydrates; 1 g fat; 0 g saturated fat; 3 g fiber; 30 g sugar; 45 mg sodium

3 small beets (beetroots)
1 cucumber
1 handful of spinach leaves
2 oranges

COCONUT WATER JUICES

On juice-only days, our Reboot plans call for drinking 16 oz of coconut water. For a more flavorful twist, try these juice additions. (But these count as your daily coconut water intake, not juice!)

Green Coconut Water (Green)

Autumn

R 🏃

+ Heart disease, diabetes, cancer, osteoporosis, inflammation/pain, autoimmune conditions, weight loss/obesity, vision, skin, immunity, memory, GI, liver, gallbladder

---

Nutrition per serving: 194 kCal; 810 kJ; 5 g protein; 40 g carbohydrates; 1 g fat; 0 g saturated fat; 1 g fiber; 24 g sugar; 44 mg sodium

4 kale (Tuscan cabbage) leaves
1 cucumber
1 celery stick
1 apple
1–2 cups/8–16 fl oz/225–450 ml coconut water

Mint Coconut Colada (Green)

Spring / Summer

 Heart disease, stroke, cancer, osteoporosis, gout, inflammation/pain, autoimmune conditions, weight loss/obesity, vision, immunity, GI

Nutrition per serving: 142 kCal; 593 kJ; 4 g protein; 29 g carbohydrates; 1 g fat; 0 g saturated fat; 1 g fiber; 20 g sugar; 71 mg sodium

¼ pineapple
2 celery sticks
1 small handful of fresh mint
1–2 cups/8–16 fl oz/225–450 ml coconut water

COCONUT WATER

Coconut water is something I didn't have on my Reboot, but I wish I'd known about it. As my nutritionist team has developed the Reboot plans, coconut water is something they've added as an essential item.

Coconut water is an important source of electrolytes, which are ions that carry electrically charged ions, including sodium, chloride, potassium, and magnesium, and are essential for the normal functioning of our cells and organs. You lose electrolytes when you sweat, and you replace them by drinking fluids.

Drinking electrolyte-rich fluids on a Reboot can help alleviate many of the side-effects commonly experienced in the first few days of the plan—feeling light-headed, dizziness, fatigue, headaches, foggy brain . . . They're also important if you have leg cramps, vomiting, or diarrhea.

But some Rebooters just don't like the taste of coconut water. If this sounds like you, I recommend mixing it with juice. So we've come up with a few special recipes for "flavored" coconut water just for you.

Strawberry on the Vine Coconut Water (Green)

Summer

+ Heart disease, stroke, high cholesterol, diabetes, cancer, osteoporosis, gout, allergies, inflammation/pain, vision, skin, immunity, GI, menstrual/ PMS/menopause/PCOS

Nutrition per serving: 105 kCal; 441 kJ; 4 g protein; 20 g carbohydrates; 1 g fat; 0 g saturated fat; 0 g fiber; 11 g sugar; 63 mg sodium

8 strawberries
1 small handful of fresh mint
1 large handful of spinach leaves
1–2 cups/8–16 fl oz/225–450 ml coconut water

Sweet Lime Coconut Water (Orange)

Autumn / Winter

R ⊙ 🏃

➕ Heart disease, high cholesterol, diabetes, arthritis, gout, migraines, autoimmune conditions, weight loss/obesity, vision, skin, immunity, GI, liver, menstrual/PMS/menopause/PCOS, gallbladder

---

Nutrition per serving: 144 kCal; 601 kJ; 4 g protein; 31 g carbohydrates; 1 g fat; 0 g saturated fat; 1 g fiber; 12 g sugar; 70 mg sodium

1 sweet potato (kumara)
½ lime
1–2 cups/8–16 fl oz/225–450 ml coconut water

SMOOTHIES

Remember, a smoothie is made in a blender; for the difference
between juicing and blending, see page 32.
Note: All smoothies make 16–18 fl oz/500 ml.

Berries & Beet

Summer

Heart disease, cancer, gout, inflammation/pain, autoimmune
conditions, vision, skin, immunity, liver

Nutrition per serving: 220 kCal; 920 kJ; 6 g protein; 50 g carbohydrates; 1.5 g fat;
0 g saturated fat; 13 g fiber; 33 g sugar; 340 mg sodium

1 cup/8 fl oz/225 ml coconut water
1 cup/4 oz/110 g raspberries, fresh or frozen
1 cup/4 oz/110 g cherries, fresh or frozen
1 cup/4½ oz/110 g strawberries, fresh or frozen
1 tablespoon goji berries (optional)
½–1 small beet (beetroot), peeled
½ small carrot
Ice (optional)

Cucumber Melon

Summer

R

+ Stroke, cancer, arthritis, gout, inflammation/pain, thyroid, weight loss/obesity, vision, skin, immunity, GI, menstrual/PMS/menopause/PCOS

Nutrition per serving: 120 kCal; 502 kJ; 3 g protein; 30 g carbohydrates; 0.5 g fat; 0 g saturated fat; 3 g fiber; 24 g sugar; 400 mg sodium

¼ honeydew melon
½ cucumber
1 celery stick
Juice of ½ lime
Pinch of sea salt (optional)
Ice (optional)

Fire Engine Red

Autumn / Winter

Heart disease, stroke, high cholesterol, cancer, osteoporosis, arthritis, inflammation/pain, autoimmune conditions, thyroid, vision, skin, immunity, liver, menstrual/PMS/menopause/PCOS

Nutrition per serving: 400 kCal; 1,672 kJ; 10 g protein; 89 g carbohydrates; 4 g fat; 1 g saturated fat; 19 g fiber; 65 g sugar; 490 mg sodium

1 cup/8 oz/230 g pomegranate seeds
2 tablespoons goji berries (optional)
½ small beet (beetroot), peeled
1½ cups/13 fl oz/375 ml coconut water

Ginger Joy

Summary

Heart disease, high cholesterol, diabetes, cancer, osteoporosis, arthritis, gout, allergies, migraines, inflammation/pain, autoimmune conditions, vision, GI, menstrual/PMS/menopause/PCOS

Nutrition per serving: 200 kCal; 836 kJ; 8 g protein; 45 g carbohydrates; 0.5 g fat; 0 g saturated fat; 12 g fiber; 28 g sugar; 330 mg sodium

1 cucumber
1 handful of spinach leaves
1 green apple, cored
1 handful of fresh parsley
1 in/2.5 cm piece of fresh ginger root
1 cup/8 fl oz/225 ml coconut water

Great Green Pear

Autumn

R

+ High cholesterol, thyroid, cancer, skin, GI, osteoporosis

Nutrition per serving: 413 kCal; 837 kJ; 6 g protein; 74 g carbohydrates; 16 g fat; 2 g saturated fat; 22 g fiber; 38 g sugar; 62 mg sodium

2 pears, juiced
2 handfuls of spinach
½ cucumber, juiced
½ avocado
1 in/2.5 cm piece of lemongrass stalk, chopped (remove outer layer)

1. Several hours before making the smoothie, juice the cucumber, pour the juice into an ice cube tray, and freeze. (Using frozen juice instead of regular ice cubes avoids a watery smoothie!)
2. Juice the pears.
3. Add the pear juice, spinach, avocado, lemongrass, and frozen cucumber cubes to the blender.

Honey I Dew

Summer

	Heart disease, stroke, arthritis, gout, migraines, inflammation/pain, immunity, GI, menstrual/PMS/menopause/PCOS

Nutrition per serving: 150 kCal; 627 kJ; 3 g protein; 35 g carbohydrates; 0 g fat; 0 g saturated fat; 9 g fiber; 22 g sugar; 400 mg sodium

3 handfuls of spinach leaves (about 4 oz/110 g)
¼ honeydew melon, rind removed (about 7 oz/200 g)
1 cup/8 fl oz/225 ml coconut water
1 handful of ice (3 to 4 cubes)

Pink Pom-Pom

Winter

+ Heart disease, diabetes, cancer, osteoporosis, arthritis, gout, allergies, migraines, inflammation/pain, vision, immunity, memory, liver

Nutrition per serving: 350 kCal; 1,463 kJ; 9 g protein; 78 g carbohydrates; 4 g fat; 1 g saturated fat; 18 g fiber; 57 g sugar; 280 mg sodium

1 cup/8 oz/230 g pomegranate seeds
1 navel orange, peeled
1 cup/8 fl oz/225 ml coconut water
1 large handful of spinach leaves

Put the Lime in the Coconut

Spring

R

+ Heart disease, stroke, high cholesterol, diabetes, cancer, gout, vision, immunity, memory, GI, menstrual/PMS/menopause/PCOS

Nutrition per serving: 140 kCal; 585 kJ; 4 g protein; 34 g carbohydrates; 1 g fat; 0.5 g saturated fat; 7 g fiber; 16 g sugar; 330 mg sodium

Juice of 1 lime
1 cup/8 fl oz/225 ml coconut water
½ banana
2 handfuls of spinach leaves
1 handful of ice (3 or 4 cubes)

Raz-Avocado

Summer

R

➕ Heart disease, stroke, high cholesterol, diabetes, cancer, arthritis, gout, allergies, thyroid, vision, skin, immunity, memory

---

Nutrition per serving: 320 kCal; 1,338 kJ; 7 g protein; 42 g carbohydrates; 16 g fat; 2.5 g saturated fat; 20 g fiber; 14 g sugar; 270 mg sodium

1¼ cups/5 oz/150 g raspberries, fresh or frozen
1½ cups/7 oz/200 g strawberries, fresh or frozen
½ avocado
1 handful of rocket (arugula)
1 cup/8 fl oz/225 ml coconut water

Sweet Basil

Spring / Summer

 Heart disease, high cholesterol, diabetes, cancer, osteoporosis, inflammation/pain, thyroid, vision, immunity, memory

Nutrition per serving: 200 kCal; 836 kJ; 8 g protein; 45 g carbohydrates; 0.5 g fat; 0 g saturated fat; 8 g fiber; 32 g sugar; 270 mg sodium

¼ pineapple, cored and skin removed
1 cucumber
1 handful of fresh basil
1 cup/8 fl oz/225 ml coconut water
1 handful of ice (3 or 4 cubes)

Sweet Bunny Love

Autumn / Winter

✚ Stroke, vision, skin, immunity, exercise, migraine, allergy, high blood pressure, thyroid

---

Nutrition per serving: 321 kCal; 837 kJ; 6 g protein; 78 g carbohydrates; 1 g fat; 0 g saturated fat; 17 g fiber; 33 g sugar; 212 mg sodium

1 large sweet potato, juiced
4 carrots, juiced
1 banana
1 date, pitted
Pinch of cinnamon

1. Several hours before making the smoothie, juice the sweet potato, pour the juice into an ice cube tray, and freeze. (Using frozen juice instead of regular ice cubes avoids a watery smoothie!)
2. Juice the carrots.
3. Add the carrot juice, frozen sweet potato cubes, banana, and date to the blender.
4. Add cinnamon to taste.

SALADS

Avocado Caprese Salad

Summer

R ◔

+ Heart disease, stroke, high cholesterol, diabetes, cancer, arthritis, gout, migraines, inflammation/pain, thyroid, vision, skin, immunity, memory, menstrual/PMS/menopause/PCOS

Serves 2 as a light meal, 4 as an appetizer

Nutrition per serving: 240 kCal; 1,003 kJ; 4 g protein; 16 g carbohydrates; 20 g fat; 3 g saturated fat; 10 g fiber; 6 g sugar; 20 mg sodium

2 large heirloom tomatoes (or any variety if heirlooms aren't available)
½ avocado
8–16 fresh basil leaves
2 tablespoons olive oil
2 tablespoons balsamic vinegar, to taste
Dash of Himalayan salt and freshly ground pepper, to taste

1. Wash the tomatoes well and cut off the ends. Then slice each one into four thick slices.

2. Slice the avocado, assemble the tomato slices on a plate, and top with the avocado (about two slices per tomato).

3. Add 1–2 basil leaves to each tomato, drizzle with olive oil and balsamic vinegar, and sprinkle with Himalayan salt and freshly ground pepper.

4. Serve as an appetizer or a light meal.

Chopped Cranberry & Collards Salad

Autumn / Winter

R ⏱

+ Diabetes, osteoporosis, gout, allergies, inflammation/pain, thyroid, vision, skin, immunity, memory, menstrual/PMS/menopause/PCOS, gallbladder

---

Serves 4

Nutrition per serving: 90 kCal; 376 kJ; 2 g protein; 23 g carbohydrates; 0 g fat; 0 g saturated fat; 5 g fiber; 14 g sugar; 10 mg sodium

1 bunch of collard greens/16 leaves (save the stems for your next green juice)
1 orange, plus 1 tablespoon orange zest
1 apple (honeycrisp or other sweet variety works best)
2 cups/7 oz/200 g fresh or frozen cranberries
1 tablespoon honey (optional)

1. Remove the collard green leaves from stems and chop. Place into a bowl.
2. Zest the orange, and then peel.
3. Juice the orange and the apple.
4. Place the cranberries and honey (if using) into a food processor and pulse for a coarse chop, adding the orange/apple juice in small batches.
5. Pour the cranberry/orange/apple dressing over the collards, sprinkle the orange peel over the salad, and then serve immediately.

Colorful Cold Weather Salad

Autumn / Winter

➕ Cancer, arthritis, gout, inflammation/pain, vision, skin, immunity, memory, liver, menstrual/PMS/menopause/PCOS, gallbladder

---

Serves 4

Nutrition per serving: 210 kCal; 878 kJ; 7 g protein; 32 g carbohydrates; 8 g fat; 1 g saturated fat; 8 g fiber; 8 g sugar; 100 mg sodium

1 butternut squash, chopped into small cubes
1 large beet (beetroot) or 2 small beets, peeled and chopped into small cubes
1 cup/4 oz/110 g brussels sprouts, sliced in half
1 tablespoon coconut oil
1 bunch of kale (Tuscan cabbage) leaves
2 tablespoons olive oil
2 tablespoons balsamic vinegar

1. Preheat the oven to 450°F/230°C/gas 8.
2. Put the chopped squash, beet and brussels sprouts on a large baking pan, drizzle the coconut oil (if your kitchen is cool, you may need to melt the solid coconut oil first by standing the jar in hot water) over the veggies, and toss to coat. Cook for 45 minutes, until the veggies are tender.
3. While the other veggies are cooking, remove the kale leaves from their stems and tear into small bite-sized pieces. Add to a large bowl.
4. Combine the olive oil and balsamic vinegar in a small bowl and set aside.
5. When the veggies are done cooking, add them to the kale and toss well. Then add the dressing and toss again. Serve warm.

Evergreen Salad

Winter

Heart disease, stroke, high cholesterol, cancer, osteoporosis, arthritis, migraines, autoimmune conditions, vision, immunity, memory, liver, gallbladder

---

Serves 2

Nutrition per serving: 200 kCal; 836 kJ; 5 g protein; 30 g carbohydrates; 8 g fat; 1 g saturated fat; 9 g fiber; 14 g sugar; 110 mg sodium

4 kale (Tuscan cabbage) leaves
4 large handfuls of spinach leaves
6 kumquats or 3 clementines
½ cup/4 oz/110 g pomegranate seeds
1 tablespoon olive oil
2 tablespoons balsamic vinegar

1. Remove the kale leaves from the stem and tear into small bite-sized pieces. Toss with the spinach in a large bowl to combine.
2. Slice the kumquats into thin circles and add with pomegranate seeds to the bowl.
3. Combine the olive oil and balsamic vinegar in a small bowl and stir. Pour over the salad and toss to coat the leaves. Let sit in the fridge for at least 15 minutes so the salad wilts a bit.
4. Serve on two plates and enjoy!

Fresh Fennel and Avocado Salad

Summary / Autumn

✚ Heart disease, stroke, high cholesterol, diabetes, cancer, arthritis, gout, migraines, inflammation/pain, vision, immunity, memory, GI

Serves 1

Nutrition per serving: 430 kCal; 1,797 kJ; 9 g protein; 43 g carbohydrates; 29 g fat; 4 g saturated fat; 17 g fiber; 18 g sugar; 115 mg sodium

½ orange
½ avocado
6 romaine (cos) lettuce leaves
¼ head of a small red cabbage, thin sliced
¼ of a bulb of fennel, thin sliced

For the dressing (makes enough for 4 servings)

1 handful of fresh basil leaves
1 garlic clove, chopped
2 teaspoons honey (optional)
4 tablespoons olive oil
Juice from ½ lemon
1 tablespoon apple cider vinegar
Sea salt and freshly ground pepper, to taste

1. Peel the orange and separate into sections, removing the white pith.

2. Cut the avocado in half, remove the flesh of one half with a spoon and then slice. Put the other half, with the pit in it, in the refrigerator for use in another meal.

3. Next make the dressing. Place the basil leaves into a blender or food processor with the garlic and then add the honey, olive oil, lemon juice, vinegar, and salt and pepper. Blend until smooth.

4. Chop the lettuce and transfer to a bowl. Then add the cabbage, fennel, orange, and avocado to the bowl and mix well.

5. Toss with about 2 tablespoons of dressing. Store the remaining dressing in the refrigerator up to 5 days.

Guacamole over Greens Salad

Summer

R

+ Diabetes, cancer, migraines, inflammation/pain, weight loss/obesity, vision, skin, memory, GI, liver, menstrual/PMS/menopause/PCOS, gallbladder

Serves 4

Nutrition per serving: 160 kCal; 669 kJ; 2 g protein; 10 g carbohydrates; 14 g fat; 2 g saturated fat; 8 g fiber; 2 g sugar; 20 mg sodium

2 ripe avocados, diced
1 plum tomato, seeded and diced
¼ medium red onion, fine diced
½ jalapeño, seeded and minced
Juice of ½ lime
2 tablespoons fresh cilantro (coriander), chopped
¼ teaspoon ground cumin
Dash of cayenne pepper (or more if you prefer a lot of heat)
Kosher salt, to taste
2 large handfuls of spinach leaves

1. Wash all ingredients thoroughly and prepare as listed.
2. To make the guacamole, put all the ingredients except the spinach in a bowl and mix together using a potato masher or a fork. Season to taste.
3. Spoon the guacamole over the spinach.
4. To store the guacamole, place it in an airtight container. Cover with plastic wrap, pressing the plastic wrap on top of the guacamole, sealing out the air, and then put on the container lid. This will prevent discoloration of the avocado that results from oxidation.

Hail to Kale Salad

Summary

R

Heart disease, stroke, high cholesterol, diabetes, cancer, osteoporosis, allergies, autoimmune conditions, weight loss/obesity, vision, skin, immunity, GI, liver

---

Serves 4

Nutrition per serving: 370 kCal; 1,547 kJ; 6 g protein; 40 g carbohydrates; 23 g fat; 3 g saturated fat; 9 g fiber; 22 g sugar; 70 mg sodium

1 large head of kale (Tuscan cabbage), leaves only (save stems for juicing)
½ red onion, chopped
2 carrots, peeled and cut into thin circles
1 handful of dried cranberries or blueberries
1 red bell pepper (capsicum), seeded and chopped
1 cucumber, quartered and chopped
1 avocado, cubed
1 pint/13 oz/370 g grape tomatoes (or other variety), halved
1 large handful of goji berries (optional)
4 tablespoons olive oil
4 tablespoons lemon juice

1. Rip the kale leaves into bite-sized pieces and then add to a large salad bowl. Add all the vegetables, avocado, and berries. Mix well.
2. Combine the olive oil and lemon juice in a small bowl, pour over the salad, and toss the dressing through until thoroughly combined.
3. Place in the refrigerator to "marinate" for 10–15 minutes before serving.

Roasted Carrots & Avocado Salad

Summer / Autumn

R

+ Heart disease, stroke, high cholesterol, arthritis, migraines, vision, skin, memory, GI, liver, menstrual/PMS/menopause/PCOS, gallbladder

---

Serves 2

Nutrition per serving: 360 kCal; 1,505 kJ; 6 g protein; 27 g carbohydrates; 28 g fat; 4 g saturated fat; 11 g fiber; 8 g sugar; 110 mg sodium

4 large carrots, cut lengthwise into quarters
2 tablespoons olive oil
1 tablespoon ground cumin
1 teaspoon red pepper flakes
1 avocado, sliced
Juice of 1 lemon
½ cup/3 oz/90 g arugula (rocket)
1 bunch of spinach leaves
Sea salt and freshly ground pepper, to taste

1. Preheat the oven to 375°F/190°C/gas 5.
2. Place the carrots in a mixing bowl and add ½–1 tablespoon olive oil, cumin, red pepper flakes, salt, and pepper, and toss until the carrots are evenly coated.
3. Spread the carrots out on a roasting pan and roast in the oven for 25–30 minutes until browned. Give the carrots a stir halfway through.
4. Prepare the simple lemon dressing by mixing the lemon juice with the remaining olive oil and salt and pepper to taste.
5. Remove the carrots from the oven, combine with the greens and avocado, and toss with the dressing. Serve and enjoy!

Sweet Mango, Avocado, and Tomato Salad

Summer

R

+ Heart disease, stroke, high cholesterol, cancer, gout, migraines, inflammation/pain, autoimmune conditions, thyroid, vision, skin, immunity, memory, gallbladder

---

Serves 1

Nutrition per serving: 280 kCal; 1,170 kJ; 3 g protein; 32 g carbohydrates; 18 g fat; 2.5 g saturated fat; 8 g fiber; 23 g sugar; 10 mg sodium

½ avocado, cut into chunks

½ mango, cut into chunks

½ cup/4 oz/110 g cherry tomatoes, halved

1 tablespoon olive oil

1 tablespoon lemon juice

1 garlic clove, minced

½ tablespoon raw honey (optional)

Sea salt and freshly ground pepper, to taste

1. Prepare the avocado, mango, and cherry tomatoes as listed, and mince the garlic.
2. Put the avocado, mango chunks, and halved cherry tomatoes into a large bowl.
3. In a separate bowl, combine the olive oil, lemon juice, garlic, honey (if using), and salt and pepper, and stir until evenly mixed. Pour this dressing over the salad and toss well.
4. Store the salad in the fridge for 1 hour or longer before serving.

Watermelon Mint Salad

Summer

R

+ Heart disease, diabetes, cancer, osteoporosis, migraines, vision, immunity, memory, GI, menstrual/PMS/menopause/PCOS

Serves 2

Nutrition per serving: 340 kCal; 1,421 kJ; 7 g protein; 54 g carbohydrates; 15 g fat; 2 g saturated fat; 8 g fiber; 36 g sugar; 95 mg sodium

4 large handfuls of spinach leaves
¼ watermelon, cut into small cubes
1 large handful of fresh mint
½ cup/4 oz/110 g sugar snap peas, cut into bite-sized pieces
Juice of 1 lime
1 tablespoon lime zest
2 tablespoons olive oil

1. Put the spinach, watermelon, mint, and sugar snap peas into a large bowl.
2. Zest the lime and then juice it.
3. In a separate bowl, combine the olive oil, lime juice, and lime zest, and mix well. Pour the dressing over the salad ingredients and toss well to combine.
4. Place in the fridge.
5. Serve chilled.

Wilted Kale and Summer Squash Salad with Parsley Gremolata

Summer

R

Heart disease, stroke, high cholesterol, diabetes, cancer, osteoporosis, allergies, inflammation/pain, autoimmune conditions, weight loss/obesity, skin, immunity, memory, liver, gallbladder

Serves 4

Nutrition per serving: 140 kCal; 585 kJ; 10 g protein; 29 g carbohydrates; 2 g fat; 0 g saturated fat; 7 g fiber; 7 g sugar; 105 mg sodium

1 head of kale (Tuscan cabbage), stems removed, leaves roughly chopped

1 large yellow squash, cut into circles or half moons

1 large zucchini (courgette), cut into circles or half moons

2 garlic cloves, minced

2 big handfuls of fresh parsley, finely chopped

Juice of 1 lemon

Sea salt and freshly ground pepper, to taste

1. Place the kale leaves in a large skillet with a small amount of water, cover, and steam until wilted, about 3–5 minutes.
2. Once the leaves are wilted, add the squash and zucchini (courgette) to the pan and cook over medium heat until the squash is just tender, about 5–7 minutes. Transfer to a bowl.
3. Fine chop and mix together the garlic, parsley, and lemon juice, salt, and pepper.
4. Dress the kale and squash with the parsley gremolata and serve warm or at room temperature.

SOUPS

Cauliflower Soup

Summer / Autumn

R ⊙

✚ Heart disease, cancer, allergies, autoimmune conditions, liver, gallbladder

---

Serves 4

Nutrition per serving: 120 kCal; 502 kJ; 3 g protein; 13 g carbohydrates; 7 g fat; 1 g saturated fat; 4 g fiber; 6 g sugar; 480 mg sodium

4 cups/32 fl oz/1 liter low-sodium vegetable broth
1 head of cauliflower, cut into small florets
2 tablespoons extra virgin olive oil
1 yellow onion, chopped
1 tsp coconut or olive oil, for sauteeing
Dash of Himalayan salt and freshly ground black pepper, to taste

1. Bring the vegetable broth to a boil in a large pan, add the cauliflower florets and the olive oil, and cook for at least 10 minutes, until soft.

2. While the cauliflower is cooking, sauté the onion in coconut or olive oil until translucent, about 5 minutes.

3. When cooked, transfer cauliflower mixture and onion to a blender in batches, and puree or use an immersion blender.

4. Return soup to pot and heat over medium for a few minutes.

5. Serve in small bowls. Add a drizzle of olive oil (optional) and a sprinkle of Himalayan salt and freshly ground pepper, to desired taste.

Creamy Parsnip Soup

Autumn / Winter

✚ Heart disease, cancer, allergies, autoimmune conditions, liver, gallbladder

---

Serves 6

Nutrition per serving: 210 kCal; 878 kJ; 3 g protein; 41 g carbohydrates; 5 g fat; 1 g saturated fat; 9 g fiber; 15 g sugar; 170 mg sodium

1 head of garlic
2 tablespoons olive oil, plus a drizzle
1 large white onion, diced
2 celery stalks, diced
½ teaspoon kosher salt
1¾ lbs/900 g parsnips, peeled and chopped into 2 in/5 cm chunks
1 large russet potato, peeled and chopped into 2 in/5 cm chunks
6 cups/4¼ pints/1½ liters low-sodium vegetable stock
3 bay leaves
Kosher salt and freshly ground white pepper, to taste
Paprika, for dusting

1. Preheat the oven to 400°F/200°C/gas 6.
2. Cut the top off of the head of garlic, exposing the cloves. Place cut side up on a piece of aluminum foil. Drizzle the exposed cloves with a bit of olive oil, and then wrap the foil over the garlic head and seal, making a package. Place in the oven and roast for 25 minutes.

3. Unwrap the foil and let the garlic cool. When cool enough to handle, squeeze the softened cloves out of their skin. Set aside 6 cloves for the soup and refrigerate the rest for another use.

4. While the garlic is cooking, heat 2 tablespoons of olive oil in a large pan over medium heat. Add the onion, celery, and salt, and sauté until the vegetables are soft and translucent, about 5 minutes.

5. Add the parsnips, potato, vegetable stock, and bay leaves, and bring to a boil. Reduce the heat, cover, and let the soup simmer until the vegetables are very soft, about 45 minutes.

6. Remove the bay leaves and let the soup cool slightly. Transfer the soup to a blender. Add the roasted garlic cloves and puree. (Be careful—the soup is hot!) Or add the roasted garlic to the pot and puree with an immersion blender. Season with the kosher salt and white pepper to taste.

7. To serve, portion the soup into bowls and dust with the paprika.

Fierce Carrot Avocado Soup

Summer / Autumn

R ⏱

+ Heart disease, stroke, cancer, arthritis, migraines, inflammation/pain, thyroid, skin, immunity, vision

---

Serves 4

Nutrition per serving: 290 kCal; 1,214 kJ; 6 g protein; 52 g carbohydrates; 8 g fat; 1 g saturated fat; 14 g fiber; 17 g sugar; 450 mg sodium

2½ cups/20 fl oz/½ liter fresh organic carrot juice

1½ large avocados (½ for garnish)

1 tablespoon of fresh ginger, minced

½ teaspoon garlic, chopped

¼ teaspoon cayenne (or more to taste)

1 tablespoon of lemon juice

1 jalapeño pepper, seeded

5 fresh sweet mint leaves, stems removed

15–20 medium-sized basil leaves, stems removed

Dash of pink Himalayan salt

1. Place all the ingredients in your blender.
2. Puree until smooth.
3. Taste and adjust seasoning to suit you, and warm on stovetop. If it's a sweltering summer day, you can serve at room temp or slightly chilled.
4. Garnish with sliced avocado and a mint or basil leaf.

(Thank you to Reboot success story Angela Von Buelow, cohost of JuicingRadio.com, for this recipe.)

Spicy Roots Soup

Autumn / Winter

Heart disease, cancer, arthritis, gout, allergies, migraines, inflammation/pain, autoimmune conditions, weight loss/obesity, vision, immunity, liver, menstrual/PMS/menopause/PCOS, gallbladder

---

Serves 6

Nutrition per serving: 250 kCal; 1,045 kJ; 6 g protein; 29 g carbohydrates; 13 g fat; 2 g saturated fat; 7 g fiber; 10 g sugar; 190 mg sodium

2 tablespoons olive oil

1 large sweet onion, diced

1 leek, chopped

5 garlic cloves, chopped

1 large sweet potato, peeled and cubed

2 large parsnips, peeled and chopped

5 large carrots, peeled and chopped

¼ jalapeño, seeded and minced (optional)

8 cups/70 fl oz/2 liters low-sodium vegetable broth

1–2 tablespoons curry powder

1 teaspoon turmeric

4 in/10 cm piece of fresh ginger root, peeled and grated

3 tablespoons fresh sage, chopped

Black pepper, to taste

1. Heat the olive oil in a heavy pot over medium heat. Sauté the onion, leek, and garlic until softened, about 5 minutes. You do not want to brown the onion or garlic.

2. Add the sweet potato, parsnips, carrots, jalapeño, and spices, and then the vegetable broth and water. Simmer covered until the vegetables are soft (your fork should be able to easily pierce through), about 30 minutes.

3. Transfer to a blender in batches and puree or use an immersion blender.

4. Add soup back to the pot and warm on medium for a few minutes.

5. Serve warm.

Summertime Watermelon Gazpacho

Summer

R

+ Heart disease, stroke, cancer, arthritis, migraines, inflammation/pain, thyroid, weight loss, skin, PCOS/menstrual

Serves 6

Nutrition per serving: 168 kCal; 703 kJ; 3 g protein; 18 g carbohydrates; 11 g fat; 1 g saturated fat; 3 g fiber; 12 g sugar; 201 mg sodium

1½ lbs/680 g seedless watermelon, coarsely chopped

1½ lbs/680 g ripe summer tomatoes, diced

2 small cucumbers, peeled and coarsely chopped

1 handful of fresh basil leaves, coarsely chopped

4 tablespoons olive oil

¼ medium red onion, coarsely chopped

2 medium garlic cloves, coarsely chopped

2 tablespoons red wine vinegar

1½ teaspoons Himalayan salt

½ teaspoon whole cumin seeds (optional)

⅛ teaspoon cayenne pepper (optional)

The garnish

½ cup/40 g diced organic cucumber

½ cup/70 g diced seedless watermelon

Fresh basil

Olive oil

1. Toss all ingredients in a large bowl until evenly coated and let marinate for 20 minutes.

2. Add mixture to blender in batches and puree, or use an immersion blender, adding water as needed until desired consistency is attained.

3. Place in the refrigerator for at least 30 minutes prior to serving.

4. Serve chilled with suggested garnish.

(Thank you to Reboot success story Angela Von Buelow, cohost of JuicingRadio.com, for this recipe.)

SIDES

Caprese Kale Sauté

Summary... *Summer*

+ Heart disease, stroke, high cholesterol, diabetes, cancer, osteoporosis, gout, allergies, migraines, autoimmune conditions, vision, skin, immunity, memory, liver, menstrual/PMS/menopause/PCOS, gallbladder

---

Serves 2

Nutrition per serving: 60 kCal; 251 kJ; 3 g protein; 9 g carbohydrates; 3 g fat; 0 g saturated fat; 2 g fiber; 1 g sugar; 30 mg sodium

3 teaspoons olive oil
2 garlic cloves, chopped
½ cup/4 oz/110 g cherry tomatoes, halved
2 cups/14 oz/450 g kale (Tuscan cabbage) leaves
½ teaspoon dried basil
Dash of sea salt and pepper, to taste

1. Warm a sauté pan over medium heat and add the olive oil. Sauté the tomatoes for about 5 minutes and add the garlic. Cook until fragrant, about 3 minutes.

2. Add kale, stir, cover the pan, and continue to cook for about 5 minutes or until the kale is cooked but not wilted. Add the salt, pepper, and basil to the pan, and mix well to combine.

3. Remove the pan from the heat and serve immediately.

Crispy Kale Chips

Winter / Spring / Summer / Autumn

R ⏱

Heart disease, stroke, high cholesterol, diabetes, cancer, osteoporosis, gout, allergies, migraines, inflammation/pain, vision, skin, immunity, memory, liver, menstrual/PMS/menopause/PCOS, gallbladder

Serves 4

Nutrition per serving: 90 kCal; 376 kJ; 2 g protein; 7 g carbohydrates; 7 g fat; 1 g saturated fat; 1 g fiber; 0 g sugar; 200 mg sodium

1 bunch of kale (Tuscan cabbage), stems removed, torn into large pieces
2 tablespoons olive oil
Sea salt, to taste

1. Preheat the oven to 300°F/150°C/gas 2.
2. Toss the kale and olive oil together in a large bowl; sprinkle with salt. Spread on a baking sheet in a single layer and bake for 15 minutes or until crisp.
3. Spread kale on a baking sheet in a single layer and bake for 15 minutes, or until crisp.

Garam Masala Collard (Spring) Greens

Spring

R ○

✚ Cancer, arthritis, weight loss, inflammation/pain, diabetes, PCOS, vision, skin, immunity, liver, osteoporosis, GI

Serves 2

Nutrition per serving: 370 kCal; 1,003 kJ; 11 g protein; 26 g carbohydrates; 4 g fat; 0 g saturated fat; 16 g fiber; 2 g sugar; 90 mg sodium

2 bunches/2 lbs/900 g collard greens (cabbage leaves), ribs removed and chopped
1½ teaspoons garam masala*
1 teaspoon turmeric
4 tablespoons grape-seed oil, olive oil, or coconut oil
2 tablespoons mustard seed oil
1 teaspoon sea salt or Himalayan salt
6 tablespoons fresh cilantro (coriander), chopped

1. Heat a large saucepan or Dutch oven over medium-high heat.
2. Add the garam masala and turmeric, and heat until fragrant, about 2 minutes, stirring to make sure that the spices do not burn.
3. Add both oils to the pan, stirring to make sure that the spices and oils completely mix.
4. Add the collard greens and salt, and toss to coat with the oil.
5. Cover the pan and cook until the greens are wilted, about 5 minutes.
6. Remove from the heat and mix in the chopped cilantro.

Garam masala: store bought or as follows

2 tablespoons each of cumin, coriander, and cardamom seeds

1 teaspoon whole cloves

2 tablespoons black peppercorns

1 small cinnamon stick

1. Grind all the ingredients in a spice grinder or using a mortar and pestle.

Garlic Cauliflower Mash

Summer / Autumn

✚ Arthritis, allergies, migraines, inflammation/pain, autoimmune conditions, weight loss/obesity, immunity, memory, liver, gallbladder

---

Serves 4

Nutrition per serving: 100 kCal; 418 kJ; 2 g protein; 9 g carbohydrates; 7 g fat; 3 g saturated fat; 3 g fiber; 4 g sugar; 50 mg sodium

1 head of cauliflower, cut into small florets
1 tablespoon olive oil
2 garlic cloves, chopped
2 tablespoons coconut oil
1 teaspoon fresh chives, chopped
1 teaspoon paprika
½ teaspoon each of sea salt and freshly ground black pepper

1. Preheat the oven to 425°F/220°C/gas 7.
2. Place the cauliflower on a baking sheet lined with parchment paper. Drizzle olive oil over the cauliflower, and add a pinch of salt and pepper. Place in the oven and roast for 20 minutes or until slightly browned.
3. Puree the roasted cauliflower, garlic, coconut oil, and the remaining salt and pepper in a blender or food processor.
4. Serve garnished with chives and a sprinkle of paprika.

Roasted Pear and Brussels Sprouts

Autumn / Winter

R

+ Heart disease, stroke, high cholesterol, cancer, osteoporosis, arthritis, inflammation/pain, weight loss/obesity, immunity, memory, GI, liver, menstrual/PMS/menopause/PCOS

Serves 2

Nutrition per serving: 180 kCal; 334 kJ; 6 g protein; 29 g carbohydrates; 3.5 g fat; 0 g saturated fat; 8 g fiber; 14 g sugar; 70 mg sodium

2 cups/7 oz/200 g brussels sprouts, stems removed and cut in half
½ medium pear, cut into small cubes
1 teaspoon olive oil
1 tablespoon dried cranberries
Dash of salt and freshly ground pepper, to taste

1. Preheat the oven to 425°F/220°C/gas 7.
2. Place the brussels sprouts and pear into a glass baking dish lined with aluminum foil. Add the olive oil, salt, and pepper.
3. Roast in the oven, stirring the mixture every 5–10 minutes for about 25 minutes or until the brussels sprouts are tender and browned. Remove from the oven, add the cranberries, and serve!

MAINS

Baked Zucchini with Herbs

Summer

R

+ High-cholesterol, cancer, gout, inflammation/pain, autoimmune conditions, thyroid, weight loss/obesity, vision, skin, immunity, GI, menstrual/PMS/menopause/PCOS

Serves 4

Nutrition per serving: 190 kCal; 795 kJ; 4 g protein; 13 g carbohydrates; 14 g fat; 2 g saturated fat; 4 g fiber; 9 g sugar; 45 mg sodium

5 small zucchini (courgettes)
4 scallions, chopped, white and green parts separated
1 small onion, chopped
2 plum tomatoes, seeded and coarsely chopped
2 tablespoons celery leaves (from inner stalks), chopped
4 tablespoons basil leaves, chopped, plus extra for garnish
¼ cup/4 oz/125 ml olive oil
1 teaspoon sea salt
½ teaspoon freshly ground black pepper

1. Preheat oven to 425°F/220°C/gas 7.

2. Slice the zucchini in half crosswise. Cut each half again lengthwise, and cut or mandoline into ¼ in/.5 cm sticks.

3. In a bowl, mix together the zucchini sticks, the white parts of the scallions, onion, tomatoes, celery leaves, and basil.

4. Mix in the olive oil, salt, and pepper, and toss to combine.

5. Pour into a 3-quart baking dish and bake for 20 minutes.

6. Garnish with the chopped green tops of the scallions and the extra chopped basil.

Stuffed Winter Pumpkin

Winter

✚ Heart disease, stroke, high cholesterol, cancer, osteoporosis, arthritis, allergies, inflammation/pain, vision, skin, immunity, memory, GI, liver, menstrual/PMS/menopause/PCOS, gallbladder

---

Serves 2

Nutrition per serving: 200 kCal; 836 kJ; 8 g protein; 33 g carbohydrates; 6 g fat; 1 g saturated fat; 7 g fiber; 11 g sugar; 60 mg sodium

1 small to medium sugar pumpkin, top cut off and seeds removed
½ medium yellow onion, chopped
½ cup/4 oz/110 g cherry tomatoes, halved
½ cup/1½ oz/40 g white or baby bella mushrooms, sliced
1 handful of spinach leaves
4 large brussels sprouts, halved
½ teaspoon dried basil, crushed
Olive oil, to drizzle
Sea salt and freshly ground black pepper, to taste

1. Preheat the oven to 350°F/180°C/gas 4.
2. Place the onion, tomatoes, mushrooms, spinach, and brussels sprouts in a mixing bowl. Drizzle with olive oil, sprinkle with salt and pepper, and scatter the basil. Stuff all the ingredients into the pumpkin.
3. Place the stuffed pumpkin on a baking sheet lined with parchment paper and transfer to the oven. Check the pumpkin after 90 minutes to see if the vegetables are bubbling and the flesh of the pumpkin is soft. The pumpkin should be completely cooked in approximately 2 hours.
4. Serve warm.

Sweet Potato Sliders

Autumn / Winter

R

+ Heart disease, stroke, cancer, arthritis, migraines, allergies, skin, immunity, vision

---

Serves 3

Nutrition per serving: 140 kCal; 586 kJ; 2 g protein; 16 g carbohydrates; 9 g fat; 1.5 g saturated fat; 4 g fiber; 4 g sugar; 30 mg sodium

2 medium sweet potatoes, peeled and cut into uniform circles* (should have at least 24 slices)
12 baby bella mushroom caps (about the same circumference as the sweet potatoes)
Sea salt and freshly ground pepper, to taste.
Optional herbs (fresh when possible or dried): basil, oregano, Old Bay, cinnamon, cumin, chipotle, cracked red pepper
2 teaspoons olive oil

*Spread***

1 avocado
1 tablespoon olive oil
1 tablespoon water
2 cloves garlic
¼ onion
¼ teaspoon freshly ground black pepper
Pinch of sea salt (optional)
Squeeze of lime

To Serve

2 kale (Tuscan cabbage) leaves, chopped

¼ cucumber, sliced (12 slices)

1 tomato, sliced (12 slices)

¼ red onion, sliced (12 slices)

1. Preheat oven to 425°F/220°C/gas 7.
2. Peel sweet potatoes and make uniform, thick slices.
3. Remove stems from mushrooms.
4. Place mushroom caps and sweet potato slices onto separate baking sheets.
5. Drizzle olive oil over sweet potato slices and mushrooms.
6. Sprinkle herbs over sweet potato slices. Try using combinations (Old Bay + black pepper for some, basil + oregano + black pepper on others, cinnamon + cumin, chipotle + cracked red pepper).
7. Bake mushrooms 10–15 minutes until tender. Bake sweet potato slices about 20–25 minutes depending on the thickness of the slices, flipping about halfway through. Sweet potato should be cooked through but still slightly firm.
8. While the vegetables are cooking, place all spread ingredients in a blender or food processor and pulse to desired consistency.
9. When finished cooking, let sweet potato slices and mushrooms cool and drain. Mushrooms are best when drained stem-side down on a paper towel.
10. Spoon spread onto 1 sweet potato circle. Add a mushroom and top with other veggies—kale/lettuce, cucumber, tomato, onion—just like a burger! Add a little more avocado spread. Top with another sweet potato circle. Repeat the process until you've used all your sweet potatoes. You will most likely end up with leftover spread, so feel free to have some on its own or with veggies like carrots, celery, or peppers.

**For a sweeter taste try using pureed butternut squash (pumpkin) seasoned with cumin + cinnamon in place of the avocado spread.*

After your Reboot try using hummus, cashew cheese, white bean, or edamame spread along with or in place of the avocado spread for more protein.

Tomato-Basil Spaghetti Squash

Autumn

R

➕ Heart disease, stroke, high cholesterol, cancer, osteoporosis, arthritis, gout, autoimmune conditions, skin, immunity, memory, GI, menstrual/PMS/menopause/PCOS

Serves 2

Nutrition per serving: 180 kCal; 752 kJ; 6 g protein; 31 g carbohydrates; 6 g fat; 1 g saturated fat; 8 g fiber; 15 g sugar; 690 mg sodium

1 medium or large spaghetti squash, halved and seeds removed
2 teaspoons olive oil, divided
½ medium yellow onion, chopped
1 garlic clove, chopped
1 medium head of broccoli, chopped
¾ cup/5 oz/140 g cherry tomatoes, halved
½ cup/4 fl oz/120 ml organic tomato sauce (tomato puree)
Sea salt and freshly ground pepper, to taste
Fresh basil leaves, to garnish

1. Preheat the oven to 350°F/180°C/gas 4.
2. Place the squash face down onto a baking sheet, lightly coated with olive oil. Cook in the oven for about 1 hour or until soft. Remove the squash from the oven and allow to cool.
3. Heat the olive oil in a medium pan, add the chopped onion and garlic, and cook for about 5 minutes until soft. Add the broccoli and cherry tomatoes and

continue to cook, stirring occasionally until soft. Add the tomato sauce and simmer for 5 minutes, stirring occasionally.

4. Scoop the insides of the spaghetti squash into the hot pan using a fork. Fold the squash into the ingredients in the pan to coat with the sauce, and add the salt and pepper. Serve garnished with fresh basil.

Zucchini (Courgette) Noodles with Fresh & Easy Herb Tomato Sauce

Summer

R

+ Heart disease, high cholesterol, cancer, gout, inflammation/pain, autoimmune conditions, weight loss/obesity, vision, skin, memory, GI, liver, gallbladder

Serves 4

Nutrition per serving: 210 kCal; 878 kJ; 6 g protein; 20 g carbohydrates; 15 g fat; 2 g saturated fat; 6 g fiber; 12 g sugar; 45 mg sodium

Noodles

4 zucchini (courgette)
2 tablespoons olive oil
Kitchen tool: Spiralizer—A spiralizer is a tool that is used to make long ribbons from vegetables. You can pick one up at a cooking store. If you don't own a spiralizer, you can slice the zucchini in a food processor or with a mandoline, or use a sharp knife to make thin strips.

1. Slice the zucchini in half and assemble one half at a time on the spiralizer. Push them through and allow the noodles to fall into a bowl. Cut the noodles into the size that you prefer.
2. Heat olive oil in a large pan over medium-low heat. Add zucchini noodles and cook until soft, about 5–10 minutes. You don't have to cook them, but it will soften them. Drain the noodles.
3. Add tomato sauce and toss gently to blend.

Sauce

2 tablespoons olive oil

1 onion, chopped

10 tomatoes, chopped

4 garlic cloves, chopped

1 handful of fresh parsley, chopped

1 teaspoon ground cumin

1 tablespoon dried oregano

1 tablespoon dried thyme, crushed

Sea salt (about ½ teaspoon) and freshly ground pepper (½–1 teaspoon), to taste

1. Heat the oil in an iron skillet or an oven-safe pan on low-medium heat. Sauté the onion until soft. Add the tomatoes, garlic, parsley, herbs, and salt. Simmer for 5–8 minutes.

2. Serve the tomato sauce over the noodles.

PULP

Homemade Pulp Vegetable Broth

R

+ Cancer, arthritis, inflammation/pain, weight loss/obesity, immunity, GI

Nutrition per serving: 20 kCal; 84 kJ; 3 g protein; 10 g carbohydrates; 2 g fat; 0 g saturated fat; 5 g fiber; 2 g sugar; 15 mg sodium

1 teaspoon olive oil
Pulp (from making two of the juice recipes in this book)
10 cups/80 fl oz/2½ liters water
Fresh or dried herbs: chives, thyme, rosemary, oregano, basil, Old Bay, or use any
   herbs you like (try including ginger, parsley, etc.)
½ teaspoon each sea salt and freshly ground black pepper

1. Heat the olive oil in a pan over medium heat. Add the pulp and stir for 1–2 minutes. Add water, herbs, spices, and seasonings, and turn up to high heat. Bring to a boil, reduce heat, and simmer uncovered for 2–3 hours to reduce the liquid.
2. Strain with a fine mesh colander over a bowl.
3. Let cool, then sip and enjoy!

Note: Use in soup recipes. Vegetable broth is also a great substitute for water or tea when Rebooting. And it's great on a cold day.

Thai Infused Vegetable Broth

+ Cancer, pain/inflammation, immunity, weight loss, diabetes, PCOS, arthritis, thyroid

---

Nutrition per serving: 28 kCal; 105 kJ; 1g protein; 7 g carbohydrates; 0.06 g fat; 0 g saturated fat; 0 g fiber; 0 g sugar; 3 mg sodium

2 cups/7 oz/100 g of vegetable pulp
8 cups/72 fl oz/2 liters of water
2 sticks of lemongrass, chopped fine
2 cloves garlic, crushed
Fresh cilantro (coriander), chopped
Sea salt and pepper, to taste
1–2 fresh chili peppers, chopped (optional)

1. Bring water to a boil in a large pot, turn down heat, and add pulp.
2. Add lemongrass, garlic, cilantro (coriander), chili peppers, salt, and pepper.
3. Simmer covered for 2 hours.
4. Strain through a fine mesh colander over a bowl.
5. Leave to cool, and then sip and enjoy!

Note: Vegetable broth is a great substitute for water or tea when Rebooting. And it's great on a cold day.

Banana, Carrot, and Zucchini (Courgette) Muffins

Heart disease, stroke, high cholesterol, diabetes, arthritis, gout, allergies, inflammation/pain, autoimmune conditions, thyroid, vision, skin, immunity, memory

Makes 4–6 large muffins or 8–10 small ones

Nutrition per serving: 223 kCal; 933 kJ; 4 g protein; 19 g carbohydrates; 4 g fat; 1 g saturated fat; 6 g fiber; 15 g sugar; 65 mg sodium

3 flax eggs (3 tablespoons ground flaxseeds added to 9 tablespoons of water and stirred), or use 3 regular eggs and ¼ cup/1 oz/30 g coconut or almond flour
2 fresh bananas
1 cup/4oz/100 g pulp from juiced carrots and zucchini
¼ cup/2 oz/55 g coconut oil
4 dates, pitted
½ teaspoon bicarbonate of soda (baking soda)
½ teaspoon sea salt
½ cup/2 oz/60 g walnuts, chopped

1. Preheat the oven to 350°F/180°C/gas 4.
2. Combine the flax eggs (or regular eggs), bananas, pulp, coconut oil, and dates in a high-powered blender and blend until smooth. Add in the coconut flour (if using regular eggs), bicarbonate of soda (baking soda), and salt, and blend until smooth. Then fold in the walnuts.
3. Pour the mixture into a muffin pan (either grease the pan or place the mixture into muffin wrappers). Bake in the oven 30–35 minutes.

4. Remove from the oven and let sit for at least 20 minutes before serving. Slice in half and serve with your favorite nut butter, mashed-up berries, or just alone!

Note: These are easy-to-make gluten-free muffins. They will be more dense and will not rise as much as gluten muffins. The flax eggs will make the muffins even more cake-like and moist.

Black Bean & Quinoa Veggie-Pulp Burgers

+ Heart disease, stroke, high cholesterol, diabetes, osteoporosis, arthritis, gout, allergies, inflammation/pain, weight loss/obesity, skin, GI, liver, gallbladder

---

Serves 6

Nutrition per serving: 232 kCal; 971 kJ; 9 g protein; 12 g carbohydrates; 5 g fat; 1 g saturated fat; 7 g fiber; 16 g sugar; 59 mg sodium

½ cup/4 oz/125 g quinoa
1 cup/8 fl oz/225 ml water (for the quinoa)
1 BPA-free can (16 oz/450 g) black beans
1 cup pulp—use any variety, but carrot and kale are great places to start
½ cup/3 oz/80 g rolled oats
1 teaspoon chili powder
1 teaspoon ground cumin
½ teaspoon cayenne pepper
Small handful of fresh cilantro (coriander)
2 tablespoons olive oil
1 teaspoon coconut oil, for coating
1 avocado, sliced
Juice of 1 lime
Sea salt and freshly ground pepper, to taste

1. Preheat the oven to 450°F/230°C/gas 8.
2. Put the quinoa and water in a pan and bring to a boil. Reduce to a simmer and stir occasionally. Cook for about 15 minutes, until all the water is evaporated.

3. While the quinoa is cooking, rinse and drain the black beans well. Combine the beans, cooked quinoa, juice pulp, oats, chili pepper, cumin, cayenne, cilantro (coriander), salt, pepper, and olive oil in a large bowl and mix well. You can lightly mash the mixture as you stir it to make it stick together. Once well combined, make the mixture into 6 small patties.

4. Coat a baking sheet with a light layer of coconut oil and place the patties on the sheet. Drizzle the top of the patties with more oil, and bake for 12 minutes. The burgers might be a bit crispy on the outside, so cook them shorter or longer depending on your preference.

5. Once cooked, top with slices of avocado and a squeeze of fresh lime juice.

Rosemary Carrot Flax Crackers

+ Heart disease, high cholesterol, diabetes, arthritis, migraines, inflammation/pain, autoimmune conditions, thyroid, vision, skin, immunity, memory, liver, menstrual/PMS/menopause/PCOS, gallbladder

Makes about 60 small crackers; serving size is 10 crackers

Nutrition per serving: 300 kCal; 1,255 kJ; 8 g protein; 29 g carbohydrates; 22 g fat; 1 g saturated fat; 8 g fiber; 20 g sugar; 43 mg sodium

1 cup/4 oz/110 g raw flaxseeds

4 cups/16 oz/250 g raw sunflower seeds

1 cup/4 oz/113 g carrot pulp

¼ cup/1 oz/30 g raw sesame seeds

1 tablespoon garlic powder

2 tablespoons dried rosemary, chopped finely

1 teaspoon sea salt and freshly ground pepper, to taste

1 avocado (optional, to use as the cracker's spread)

1. Combine the flaxseeds with 1 cup/8 fl oz/250 ml of water and let sit for 1 hour, until it forms a gooey consistency.
2. Place the sunflower seeds and carrot pulp in a food processor and pulse until well chopped.
3. Transfer the sunflower seeds and pulp into a bowl, add the gooey flaxseeds, and stir in the sesame seeds, garlic powder, rosemary, salt, and pepper. Mix well to create a wet, crumbly mixture.
4. Spread into a thin layer on dehydrator trays lined with parchment paper. Score the crackers before dehydrating them so they snap apart easily and evenly when they are done. Leave to dehydrate for 7–8 hours at 115°F/46°C.*
5. Serve plain or add avocado as a healthy spread.

Don't have a dehydrator? Use your oven! Set your oven at its very lowest heat and leave your oven door cracked open. Place your cracker mixture onto a baking sheet lined with parchment paper and place in the oven. Leave the crackers to dry for at least 3–4 hours. Flip the crackers over and dry for another 30 minutes to 1 hour.

Veggie Meatballs

+ Heart disease, diabetes, cancer, arthritis, gout, allergies, inflammation/pain, autoimmune conditions, thyroid, skin, memory, liver, gallbladder

Serves 2

Nutrition per serving: 298 kCal; 1,247 kJ; 6 g protein; 19 g carbohydrates; 14 g fat; 1 g saturated fat; 7 g fiber; 15 g sugar; 20 mg sodium

1 cup/4 oz/100 g pulp from kale, spinach, celery, cucumber, carrots, apple

½ red bell pepper (capsicum), chopped

1 zucchini (courgette), chopped

2 garlic cloves, chopped

1 tablespoon fresh parsley, chopped

¾ tablespoon Italian seasoning

1 tablespoon olive oil

¼ cup/1 oz/30 g nutritional yeast (optional)

3 tablespoons ground flaxseed mixed with 8 tablespoons water (for binding)

1. Preheat the oven to 350°F/180°C/gas 4.
2. Sauté the pepper, zucchini, and garlic in the olive oil over medium heat. Transfer to a bowl. Mix the pulp with the sautéed vegetables, and add the flaxseed/water mixture plus Italian seasoning and parsley.
3. Form the mixture into veggie balls, and place them in a baking dish. Sprinkle the nutritional yeast over them, if using, and place the dish in the oven. Cook until golden brown, about 15 minutes.
4. Add to your favorite whole wheat, whole grain, or spinach spaghetti, and combine with a marinara sauce. If you want a lighter pasta, use a peeler or a mandoline to grate raw zucchini (courgette) for your "noodles."

Healthy Dog Treats
(That people can eat too!)

🕐

3 cups/15 oz/450 g pulp from carrot, sweet potato, apple, and spinach

½ cup/5 oz/125 g peanut butter

¼ cup/1 oz/20 g rolled oats

1 tablespoon coconut oil

1 mashed banana

1. Preheat the oven to 350°F/180°C/gas 4.
2. Mix all the ingredients together until well combined, and then roll into little cookie shapes—the size can vary depending on the size of your pet. Bake for 15 minutes.
3. Let treats cool before serving to your pet!

RESOURCES

Need inspiration for how to eat post-Reboot? There are plenty of great plant-based, raw, vegetarian, vegan, and paleo books available; check out the cooking section in any bookstore for ideas. If you want some recommendations, though, the following books are from authors who have been particularly inspiring to Rebooters. And don't forget, the Reboot Team is continually publishing new recipes to RebootwithJoe.com, so make sure to visit us!

- *Eat to Live Cookbook* by **Dr. Joel Fuhrman**—filled with excellent plant-powered recipes to maintain your good health after a Reboot.

- *Eating on the Wild Side* by **Jo Robinson**—a great resource for getting the most nutrition and flavor out of your produce; full of tips on best varieties, storage, and preparation.

- *Everyday Raw* by **Matthew Kenney**—any book from chef Matthew Kenney is sure to be great. This one in particular is a great guide to raw "cooking."

- *Giada's Feel Good Food* by **Giada De Laurentiis**—full of practical, delicious recipes for all diet types including gluten-free, vegan, vegetarian, and pescatarian.

- *It's All Good* by **Gwyneth Paltrow**—great recipes for the mainly vegan, sometime a little pescatarian.

- *Living Raw Food* by **Sarma Melngailis**—food so good you won't believe it's all raw! From one of my favorite New York City restaurants, Pure.

- *Main Street Vegan* by **Victoria Moran**—complete guide to making the dietary and lifestyle shift to a vegan diet with simple, practical steps.

FOR YOUR DOCTOR

You might like to download a PDF of the following text to give to your doctor (visit www.rebootwithjoe.com/for-your-doctor):

Most medical experts agree on and numerous studies show the benefits of consuming fresh fruits and vegetables and fresh expressed juices in the prevention and treatment of obesity, cardiovascular disease, inflammatory conditions, and cancer.

Your patient has expressed interest in starting on the path toward healthier eating by participating in a Reboot program. It is recommended that anyone with medical problems, on prescription medications, or who is interested in participating in the program for longer than 15 days consult their doctor.

What is a Reboot?

- It is a chance to break the cycle of unhealthy eating.

- It is a temporary period of time in which a person commits to eating and/or drinking only fruits and vegetables.

- It is not a diet; it is a time for the body and mind to reset and maximally absorb micronutrients and phytonutrients in order to allow for a transition to healthier whole foods and plant-rich eating behaviors.

WHY INCLUDE JUICE?

How many patients have told you they would eat more vegetables, but they just don't like the taste? Juicing overcomes this obstacle. It offers many delicious health benefits, including numerous servings of fruits and veggies in just one glass and the immune-boosting nutrients and phytochemicals naturally found in freshly extracted juice. Most commercial juices are highly processed and lack nutrition compared to freshly juiced fruits and vegetables.

REBOOT BASICS

- Reboot length can vary from 3 to 60 days.

- Guidelines are provided online to help individuals decide which Reboot program is best for them, and all the information needed is available free of charge at www.rebootwithjoe.com.

- Individual and group support from credentialed nutritionists at respected academic institutions is available in Guided Reboots for a reasonable fee.

- Fruits and vegetables are the principal components of a Reboot, followed by guidelines for other healthy food choices after the completion of a Reboot.

- Many people find that replacing breakfast and lunch with a nutrient-packed fresh fruit juice or smoothie, along with a healthy dinner, results in significant improvements in eating habits, health, and weight.

Protein

A Reboot is not meant to be a long-term meal plan. Plant-based protein is present in the foods eaten during a Reboot. Because this is a short-term change designed ultimately to lead to healthier eating habits, protein deficiencies do not typically develop. If you have concerns about your patient's protein intake during a Reboot, we have several plant-based protein supplements that we can recommend adding into their plan.

MEDICAL SUPPORT

- Medical judgment with regard to each patient is left to the discretion of the treating doctor.

- In general, no lab work is recommended for healthy individuals completing a program of up to 15 days.

- Although we have not seen any participants develop electrolyte abnormalities, we recommend that doctors check electrolytes every 15 days in those healthy individuals who are doing a juice-only Reboot for longer than 15 days.

- A juice-only Reboot is not recommended for more than 60 days, and the length of time is in part based on the BMI of the individual.

- Healthy individuals on anti-hypertensive medications have also participated in Reboots for extended periods of time, and we recommend electrolytes be checked in these individuals every 10 days. Many individuals on anti-hypertensives have been able to decrease their doses or discontinue the usage of some medications as their blood pressures normalizes. It is recommended that a patient's blood pressure is monitored during and after a Reboot and their medications adjusted as needed.

- Patients with diabetes have also successfully participated in both juice-only and juice-plus-food Reboots, with results that included decreasing and sometimes eliminating the need for medications. It is not recommended that anyone with diabetes participate without a doctor's or nutritionist's guidance.

If you have additional questions about the use of a Reboot by your patients, please email info@rebootwithjoe.com, and our nutritionists or physicians from the Medical Advisory Board will contact you. Please note that this service is intended for doctors only; due to the volume of emails, we do not respond to questions from individuals.

Free online support is provided to anyone interested in participating in a Reboot at www.rebootwithjoe.com.

INDEX

ABOUT THE AUTHOR

Joe Cross is a filmmaker, entrepreneur, author, and wellness advocate. He directed, produced, and was the subject of the award-winning documentary, *Fat, Sick & Nearly Dead*, seen by more than twenty-one million people around the world, and the popular sequel, *Fat, Sick & Nearly Dead 2*; authored *The New York Times* bestseller, *The Reboot with Joe Juice Diet* book, which has been released globally in multiple languages; and is credited with having accelerated the plant-based eating movement via media outlets including the *Wall Street Journal*, *The Times* of London and *The Dr. Oz Show*. His website, www.RebootWithJoe.com, has become an integral meeting place for a community of more than one and a half million Rebooters worldwide. His third documentary film, *The Kids Menu*, which focuses on solutions to the growing childhood obesity problem, was released in 2016.